# ARTAUD ANTHOLOGY

Antonin Artaud

# ANTHOLOGY

Edited by Jack Hirschman

City Lights Books
San Francisco

© 1965 by City Lights Books

Published by special arrangement with
Editions Gallimard, Paris
publishers of Antonin Artaud, *Ouvres Completes*
©1956, 1961 Editions Gallimard

Cover photograph: Antonin Artaud by Man Ray, 1926
Cover design by Patricia Fujii

LC Catalog Card Number 65-12730
ISBN 0-87286-000-0

Visit our website: www.citylights.com

CITY LIGHTS BOOKS are edited by Lawrence Ferlinghetti and
Nancy J. Peters and published at the City Lights Bookstore,
261 Columbus Avenue, San Francisco, CA 94133.

# Contents

# Editor's Notes + Credits

All but four of the texts in Part I of the Anthology were translated from the first volume of Gallimard's collected works of Artaud. 'No Theogony' and 'It is the act which shapes the thought . . .' were taken from the *Life and Death of the Devil Fire*. *The Journey to the Land of the Tarahumaras* and the *New Revelations of Being* were translated from the small editions in which they originally appeared. In the case of the former, I have followed Artaud's advice on the use of his letter to Henri Parisot as 'Supplement' to the *Journey*, though it should be noted that the *Journey* itself was written a decade earlier.

All the texts in Part II were translated from small editions, reviews and journals. I have taken the liberty of combining some of the poems under single headings. Thus the section entitled 'Electroshock' (my own heading) is composed of a group of individual poems and prose fragments. Similarly, I have preferred to leave Kenneth Rexroth's translations of the 'Seven Poems' in the order in which they were originally published in English, noting here, however, that the poems are individual pieces composed by Artaud at different periods during the last years of his life.

All titles are noted in the bibliography which closes the Anthology. Where a title cannot be found (as in 'Electroshock' or 'Seven Poems') the originals will be located under headings such as 'Inédits' or 'Suppôts et supplications' (extraits); for such texts belong to the very last phase of Artaud's life.

I would like to thank Bernard Frechtman for permission to reprint his translation of the 'Artaud-Rivière Correspondence', which first appeared in *Exodus* magazine; Philip Lamantia, for permission to reprint the translation of L. Dejardin of 'General Security — the Liquidation of Opium', which appeared in his book, *Narcotica*, published by the Auerhahn Press of San Francisco; Kenneth Rexroth, whose translations of 'Seven Poems' first appeared in the *Black Mountain Review;* and David Rattray, whose translation of 'There's an Old Story . . .' appeared in the *City Lights Journal.*

My thanks also to those kind enough to have read through many of the texts, offering so many helpful suggestions: to Jean Decock, Alain Cohen and Judd Hubert, in Los Angeles; to Mary Beach and Claude Pelieu, in San Francisco; to Daniele Robert and F. Teri Wehn, in Paris. And especially to Anais Nin.

Finally, my thanks to Paule Thévanin, in Paris, who has provided photostats and many rare texts, as well as photographs and editorial assistance; and to Dr. Gaston Ferdière, Pierre Chaleix and Pierre Boujut, who made possible the presentation of other photographs in this volume.

JAH

# Artaud Chronology

1896: born in Marseille, September 4

1920: comes to Paris

1923: begins correspondence with Jacques Rivière

1924-1927: takes part in surrealism; activity as stage and film actor

1927-1936: break with surrealism; development of ideas of the Theater of Cruelty; attempted realization of said theater with performance of *The Cenci*

1936: January-November in Mexico, experiments with peyote, return to France; condition shaky

1937: travel to Ireland. Aboard a boat, he is straitjacketed after threatening damage to himself, and sent by the police back to France

1937-1946: many stays in hospitals (in Rouen, Paris and Rodez). Release after nine years and return to Paris

1947: lecture in the Théatre du Vieux Colombier, January 13

1948: dies at the Hospice d'Ivry (Paris), March 4

# Correspondence with Jacques Rivière

May 1, 1923

Dear Sir,

I regret that I am unable to publish your poems in the *Nouvelle Revue Française*. But they interest me sufficiently for me to wish to make the acquaintance of their author. If you could call at the office of the review any Friday between four and six, I would be happy to see you.

Sincerely yours,

Jacques Rivière

June 5, 1923

Dear Sir,

May I, at the risk of importuning you, recur to a few matters that we discussed this afternoon?

The question of the acceptability of these poems is a problem that concerns you as well as me. I am speaking, to be sure, of their absolute acceptability, of their literary existence.

I suffer from a frightful disease of the mind. My thought abandons me at all stages. From the simple act of thinking to the external act of its materialization in words. Words, forms of phrases, inner directions of thinking, simple reactions of the mind — I am in constant pursuit of my intellectual being. Hence, whenever *I can seize upon a form*, however imperfect it may be, I hold it fast, lest I lose the entire thought. I am beneath myself, I know it, it makes me suffer, but I accept the fact in the fear of not dying entirely.

All of this, which is very badly stated, may result in a fearful misunderstanding in your judgement concerning me.

That is why — out of respect for the central feeling that dictates these poems to me and for the strong images and phrases that I have been able to find — I nevertheless offer them to existence. I have felt and accepted these phrases, these ungainly expressions which you criticize. Bear in mind: I have not questioned them. They come from the deep uncertainty of my thinking. Fortunate indeed when this uncertainty is not replaced by the absolute inexistence from which I sometimes suffer.

Here, too, I fear a misunderstanding. I would like you to realize that it is not a matter of the higher or lower existence involved in what is known as inspiration, but of a total absence, of a veritable dwindling away.

That is also why I told you that I had nothing, no work in the offing, the few things which I submitted to you being the shreds that I have managed to snatch from complete nothingness.

It is very important to me that the few manifestations of *spiritual* existence that I have been able to give myself not be regarded as inexistent because of the blotches and awkward expressions with which they are marred.

In submitting them to you, I felt that their defects, their unevenness, were not so glaring as to destroy the overall impression of each poem.

Believe me, sir, that I have no immediate or petty purpose in mind. I want only to settle a burning problem.

For I cannot hope that time or labor will remedy these obscurities or shortcomings. That is why I demand that existence so insistently and anxiously, even if it be abortive. And the question to which I would like an answer is this: do you think that a poem which is faulty but which has fine and powerful things in it can be considered to have less literary authenticity and power of action than a poem which is perfect but without great inner resonance? I recognize that a review like the *Nouvelle Revue Française* requires a certain formal excellence and a great purity of matter, but, this aside, is the substance of my thought so tangled and is its general beauty rendered so inactive by the impurities and uncertainties with which it is marred that it does not manage to exist *literally*? The entire problem of my thinking is involved. For me, it is no less than a matter of knowing whether or not I have the right to continue thinking, in verse or prose.

I shall take the liberty, some Friday in the near future, of offering you the booklet of poems, *Tric Trac du Ciel,* which has just been published by Monsieur Kahnweiler, and the little volume published by Les Contemporains, *Les Douzes Chansons.* You will then be able to let me know your *definitive* evaluation of my poems.

Antonin Artaud

### JACQUES RIVIERE TO ANTONIN ARTAUD

June 23, 1923

Dear M. Artaud,

I have read with great care what you kindly submitted to my judgement, and I think that I can, in all sincerity, reassure you with respect to the feelings of anxiety which were revealed in your letter and regarding which I was deeply touched that you chose me as confident. As I told you at the very beginning, there are awkward things and disconcerting oddities in your poems. But they seem to me to be due to a certain quest on your part rather than to lack of command over your thoughts.

Obviously (and that is what prevents me, for the time being, from publishing any of your poems in the *Nouvelle Revue Française*) you do not, in general, achieve sufficient unity of impression. But I have enough experience in reading manuscripts to sense that it is not your temperament that prevents you from focusing your abilities upon a simple poetic object and that with a little patience you will succeed, even if only by the simple elimination of divergent images or features, in writing perfectly coherent and harmonious poems.

I will always be delighted to see you and talk with you and to read whatever you care to submit to me. Shall I send back to you the copy you brought me?

With all best wishes,

Jacques Rivière

January 29, 1924

Dear Sir,

You have just cause for having forgotten me. Last May I made a little confession to you. And I asked you a question. I hope you will allow me today to complete that confession, to continue it, to plumb my very depths. I am attempting to justify myself in your eyes. I care very little whether I seem to anyone to exist. The distance that separates me from myself suffices to cure me of the judgement of others. Please do not regard this as insolence, but rather as the very faithful confession, the painful statement, of a distressing state of mind.

I was annoyed with you for a long time because of your reply. I had presented myself to you as a mental case, an actual psychic anomaly, and you answered with a literary evaluation of poems which I did not care about, which I *could* not care about. I flattered myself that I had been understood by you. I now realize that I was perhaps not explicit enough, and for that too please forgive me.

I had imagined that I had won your attention, if not by the preciosity of my verse, at least by the rarity of certain phenomena of an intellectual nature owing to which these poems were not, could not be, other than what they were, although I had within me what was needed to raise them to the highest pitch of perfection. A vain statement, I am exaggerating, but intentionally.

My question was perhaps specious, but it was of you that I asked it, of you and no one else, because of the extreme sensitivity, the almost sickly perceptiveness of your mind. I flattered myself that I was bringing you a case, a definite mental case, and, curious as I thought you were about all mental deformities, all obstacles destructive of thought, I thought thereby to draw your attention to the *real* value, the initial value of my thinking and of the products of my thinking.

The dispersiveness of my poems, their formal defects, the constant sagging of my thinking, are to be attributed not to lack of practice, of mastery of the instrument I wield, of *intellectual development,* but to a central collapse of the mind, to a kind of erosion, both essential and fleeting, of my thinking, to the passing non-possession of the material gains of my development, to the abnormal separation of the elements of thought (the impulse to think, at each of the terminal stratifications of thought, including all the states, all the bifurcations of thought and form).

There is thus something that is destroying my thinking, a something which does not prevent me from being what I might be, but which leaves me, if I may say so, in abeyance. A something furtive which takes away from me the words which I have found, which diminishes my mental tension, which destroys in its substance the mass of my thinking as it evolves, which takes away from me even the memory of the devices by which one expresses oneself and which render with precision the most inseparable, most localized, most existing modulations of thought. I shall not labor the point. There is no need to describe my state.

I should like to say only as much as is needed for you finally to understand and believe me.

So grant me credit. Recognize, I beg of you, the reality of these phenomena, recognize their furtiveness, their eternal repetition, recognize that I would have written this letter before today had I not been in this state. And so once again here is my question:

Are you familiar with the subtlety, the fragility of the mind? Have I not said enough to you about the matter to prove that I have a mind that *literarily* exists, as T. exists, or E., or S., or M? Restore to my mind the concentration of its forces, the cohesion that it lacks, the constancy of its tension, the consistency of its own substance. (And all of that is objectively so little.) And tell me whether what is lacking in my poems (the old ones) may not be restored to them all at once?

Do you think that in a sound mind excitement and extreme weakness coexist and that one can both astonish and disappoint? In any case, although I can very well judge my mind, I can judge the products of my mind only insofar as they merge with it in a kind of blissful unconsciousness. That will be my criterion.

To conclude, I am sending you, I am presenting you with the latest product of my mind. As regards myself, it is worth little, although

11

more, nevertheless, than nothingness. It is a makeshift. But the question for me is whether it is better to write that or to write nothing at all.

It is you who will answer that question by accepting or rejecting this little attempt. You will judge it from the point of view of the absolute. But I wish to say that it would be a great consolation to me to think that, although not *all* of myself is as high, as dense, as broad as I, I can still be something. For that reason, sir, be truly absolute. Judge this piece of prose without regard to any question of tendency, principles, personal taste, judge it with the charity of your soul, the essential lucidity of your mind, rethink it with your heart.

It probably indicates a brain and a soul which exist, to which a certain place is due. In favor of the palpable irradiation of that soul, dismiss it only if your conscience protests with all its might, but if you have a doubt, let it be resolved in my favor.

I submit to your judgement.

Antonin Artaud

POSTCRIPT TO A LETTER IN WHICH CERTAIN LITERARY THESES OF
JACQUES RIVIERE WERE DISCUSSED

You will say to me: in order to give an opinion on matters of this kind, another mental cohesion and another perceptiveness are required. Well then, it is *my* weakness and my *absurdity* to want to write at any cost, and to express myself.

I am a man who has greatly suffered in mind, and as such I have a *right* to speak. I know how things carry on in there. I have agreed once and for all to submit to my inferiority. And yet I am not stupid. I realize that it may be necessary to think further than I do, and perhaps otherwise. I am waiting only for my brain to change, for its upper drawers to open. In an hour, and perhaps tomorrow, my thinking will have changed, but this present thought exists, I won't let my thought be lost.

**A. A.**

# A CRY

The little celestial poet
Opens the shutters of his heart.
The heavens clash. Oblivion
Uproots the symphony.

Stableman the wild house
That has you guard wolves
Does not suspect the wraths
Smouldering beneath the big alcove
Of the vault that hangs above us.

Hence silence and darkness
Muzzle all impurity
The sky strides forward
At the crossroad of sounds.

The star is eating. The oblique sky
Is opening its flight toward the heights
Night sweeps away the scraps
Of the meal that contented us.

On earth walks a slug
Which is greeted by ten thousand white hands
A slug is crawling
There where the earth vanished.

Angels whom no obscenity summons
Were homeward bound in peace
When rose the real voice
Of the spirit that called them.

The sun lower than the daylight
Volatilized all the sea.

A strange but clear dream
Was born on the clean earth.

The lost little poet
Leaves his heavenly post
With an unearthly idea
Pressed upon his hairy heart.

Two traditions met.
But our padlocked thoughts
Lacked the place required,
Experiment to be tried again.

A. A.

## ANTONIN ARTAUD TO JACQUES RIVIERE

March 22, 1924

My letter deserved at least an answer. Sir, send back my letters and manuscripts.

I would have liked to find something intelligent to say to you, in order to make clear what separates us, but no use. I am a mind still unshaped, an imbecile. Think whatever you like of me.

Antonin Artaud

## JACQUES RIVIERE TO ANTONIN ARTAUD

March 25, 1924

Dear M. Artaud,

Quite true, I agree with you, your letters deserved an answer. I have not yet been able to give you one — that is all. Please excuse me.

I am struck by something: the contrast between the extraordinary precision of your self-diagnosis and the vagueness, or at least the formlessness, of what you are endeavoring to achieve.

It was no doubt wrong of me to attempt, in my letter of last year, to reassure you at any cost. I acted like the kind of doctor who tries to cure patients by refusing to believe them, by denying the strangeness of their case, by forcibly trying to make them normal. That is a bad method. I apologize for it.

Even if I had no other evidence, your tormented, wavering, shaky handwriting, which gives the impression of being absorbed here and there by secret whirlwinds, would be sufficient to assure me of the reality of the phenomena of mental ' erosion ' of which you complain.

But how do you manage to escape from them when you try to define your difficulty? Is it that anxiety gives you the strength and clearsightedness which you lack when you yourself are not involved? Or is it the proximity of the object which you endeavor to seize that suddenly enables you to get so firm a grip? In any case, in analyzing your own mind you are remarkably and completely successful, which should restore your confidence in that mind, since it itself is the instrument that achieves this success.

There are other considerations that can also help you, not, perhaps, to hope for a cure, but at least to put up with your sickness. They are of a general kind. You speak at one point in your letter of the ' fragility of the mind.' It is superabundantly proven by the mental disturbances that are studied and classified by psychiatry. But perhaps the extent to which so-called normal thinking is the product of adventurous mechanisms has not yet been sufficiently demonstrated.

The fact that the mind exists by itself, that it has a tendency to live on its own substance, that it develops in the individual with a kind of egoism and without bothering to maintain him in harmony with the world seems, in our time, no longer open to question. In his famous *Evening with M. Teste* Paul Valéry has brilliantly dramatized the autonomy, within us, of the faculty of thinking. In itself, the mind is a kind of canker. It propagates itself; it is constantly moving out in all directions. You yourself note, as one of your torments, ' the impulse to think, at each of the terminal stratifications of thought '; the mind's outlets are unlimited in number; no idea stands in its way; no

15

idea fatigues and satisfies it. Even the temporary satisfaction which our physical functions obtain by means of exercise are unknown to it. The man who thinks expends himself utterly. It is not being romantic to say that pure thought has no issue other than death.

There is a whole body of literature — I am aware that it pre-occupies you as much as it interests me — which is the product of the immediate and, if I may say so, animal functioning of the mind. It resembles a vast field of ruins. The columns that remain standing in it are held up only by chance. Chance reigns there, as does a kind of dismal multitude. One might say that it is the most accurate and direct expression of the monster which every man carries within him, but which he usually seeks, instinctively, to fetter in the bonds of facts and experience.

But, you will say to me, is *that* what is meant by the ' fragility of the mind '? Whereas I complain of a weakness, you describe another malady which may come from an excess of strength, from an over-flow of power.

To put it more precisely, this is how I see the matter: the mind is fragile in that it needs obstacles — adventitious obstacles. If it is alone, it loses its way, it destroys itself. It seems to me that the ' men-tal erosion,' the inner larcenies, the ' destruction ' of thought ' in its substance ' which afflicts yours, have no other cause than the too great freedom you allow it. It is the absolute that throws it out of gear. In order to grow taut, the mind needs a landmark, it needs to encounter the kindly opacity of experience. The only remedy for madness is the innocence of facts.

As soon as you accept the mental sphere, you accept all mental dis-turbances and particularly all mental laxities. If by thought one means *creation,* as you seem to mean most of the time, it must, at all costs, be relative. Security, constancy and strength can be obtained only by involving the mind in something.

I am quite aware that there is a kind of intoxication in the instant of its pure emanation, in the moment when its fluid escapes directly from the brain and encounters a quantity of spaces, a quantity of stages and levels where it can spread itself. It is this quite subjective impression of utter freedom and even utter intellectual license that our 'surrealists' have tried to render in the dogma of a poetic dimension. But the punishment for this soaring follows close behind: the possible universal changes into concrete impossibilities; the phantom that is seized is avenged by twenty inner phantoms which paralyze us, which devour our spiritual substance.

Does this mean that the normal functioning of the mind should consist of servile imitation of what exists and that to think is merely to reproduce? I do not believe so. One must choose what one wishes to 'render,' and this must be something which is not only definite, not only knowable, but also unknown. In order for the mind to tap its full power, the concrete must serve as the mysterious. All successful 'thought,' all language that grips, and the words whereby one then recognizes the writer, are always the result of a compromise between a current of intelligence that emerges from him and an ignorance that befalls him, a surprise, a hindrance. The rightness of an expression always includes a remnant of hypothesis; it is necessary that the word strike a dull object — and in less time than the object can be attained by reason. But where the object, where the obstacle, is entirely lacking, the mind continues, inflexible and weak; and everything breaks up into an immense contingency.

Perhaps I am judging you both from too abstract a point of view and with preoccupations that are too personal. It seems to me, nevertheless, that your case can be explained in large part by the considerations which I have just gone into, at somewhat too great a length, and that it falls into the general scheme I have tried to outline. As long as you allow your intellectual force to pour out into the absolute, it moves in eddies, its power is dissipated, it is exposed to predatory blasts that disorganize it; but as soon as it is brought back by anxiety to your own mind and you direct it to the enigmatic object close at hand, it condenses, intensifies, becomes useful and penetrating, and brings you positive treasures ,to wit, truths that are expressed with all the relief that can make them communicable, accessible to others, hence something which transcends your suffering, your very existence, which broadens and consolidates you, which gives you the only reality that man can reasonably hope to conquer by his own powers, reality in others.

I am not programmatically optimistic, but I refuse to despair of you. My sympathy for you is very great. It was wrong of me to have allowed so long a time to go by without writing. I am keeping your poem. Send me everything you are doing.

Sincerely,

Jacques Rivière

ANTONIN ARTAUD TO JACQUES RIVIERE

May 7, 1924

Dear M. Rivière,

To get back to a discussion that is already very old, you need only imagine for a single minute that this inability to express myself is related to the most necessary needs of my life, to my most urgent expectancies — and to the suffering that follows — in order to understand that it is not for want of willingness that I renounce myself. I am on leave from poetry. It is due only to fortuitous circumstances, circumstances unrelated to my real possibilities, that I do not fulfill myself. All I need is that someone believe that I have within me the ability to crystallize things into the right form and with the right words.

I have had to wait all this time to be in a position to send you this slight note, which is clear for want of being well-written. You can draw from it the obvious conclusions.

There is one thing in your letter that remains slightly obscure to me: the use you plan to make of the poem I sent you. You have put your finger on the one side of me. Literature, in the strict sense of the word, interests me rather little. But if by chance you deem it advisable to publish the poem, please send me the proofs. It is very important to me that two or three words be changed.

With all best wishes,

Antonin Artaud

May 24, 1924

Dear M. Artaud,

An idea occurred to me which I resisted for some time, but which I find definitely attractive. Think it over. I hope it will please you. Furthermore, it still remains to be worked out. Why not publish the letter or letters you have written to me? I have just re-read again the one of January 29. It is really quite remarkable. All that would be be required is a slight transposition. I mean that we would give the writer and the recipient invented names. Perhaps I might draft a reply on the basis of the one I sent you, though it would be more fully developed and less personal. Perhaps, too, we might introduce an excerpt from your poems or from your essay on Uccello. The whole might form a little novel in letters which would be rather curious. Let me know what you think of the idea.

Sincerely,

Jacques Rivière

May 25, 1924

Dear M. Rivière,

Why lie, why try to place on the literary level a thing which is the very cry of life? Why give an appearance of fiction to what is made up of the ineradicable substance of the soul, to what is the wail of reality? Yes, your idea pleases me, it gladdens me, it gratifies me. But on condition that it give whoever reads us the impression that he is not being presented with something that has been fabricated. We have the right to lie, but not about the essence of the matter. I do not care whether or not the letters are signed with my name. But it is absolutely necessary that the reader feels that he has in his hands the elements of a true story. You would have to publish my letters from the first to the last, which would mean going back to June 1923. The

19

reader must be provided with all the material of the discussion.

A man possesses himself in flashes, and even when he does possess himself he does not quite overtake himself. He does not achieve the constant cohesion of his forces without which true creation is impossible. Nevertheless, the man exists. I mean that he has a distinct reality which enhances him. Is he to be condemned to nothingness on the pretext that he can give only fragments of himself? You yourself do not think so, and the proof is the importance you attach to these fragments. I had long since thought of suggesting that you bring them together. I dared not do so until now, and your letter responds to my desire. This shows you how pleased I am with the idea that you propose to me. I am quite aware of the jerkiness of my poems, a jerkiness which derives from the very essence of inspiration and which is due to my incorrigible inability to concentrate upon an object. Out of physical weakness, a weakness that derives from the very substance of what is called the soul and that is the emanation of our nervous force which coagulates around objects. But the entire age suffers from this weakness. Examples: Tristan Tzara, Andrè Breton, Pierre Reverdy. But in their cases, the soul is not physically affected, not substantially affected. It is affected at all points where it joins up with something else. It is not affected *outside of thought.* Where, then, does this evil come from? Is it really the atmosphere of the age, a miracle floating in the air, an evil cosmic prodigy, or the discovery of a new world, an actual enlarging of reality? Nevertheless, the fact is that they do not suffer and that I do, not only in my mind, but in my flesh, and in my everyday soul. The unrelatedness to the object which characterizes all literature is in my case an unrelatedness to life. I can truly say that I am not in the world, and this is not a mere mental attitude. My latest poems seem to me to show definite progress. Taken as a whole, are they really so unpublishable? Moreover, it matters little. I prefer to show myself as I am, in my inexistence and my uprootedness. In any case, quite a number of extracts from them could be published. I think that most of the stanzas, taken by themselves, are good. It is only when they are put together that their value is destroyed. You yourself will choose the extracts; you will arrange the letters. *In this matter I am no longer a judge.* What I insist upon chiefly is that no ambiguity be introduced as to the nature of the phenomena which I invoke in my defense. The reader must believe that it is a matter of an actual sickness and not a phenomenon of the age, of a sickness which is related to the essence of the human being and his central possibilities of expression and which is involved in an entire life. A sickness that affects the soul in its deepest reality and that infects its manifestations. The poison of being. A veritable *paralysis.* A sickness that deprives you of speech, of memory, that uproots your thinking.

I think I have said enough to make myself understood. Publish this last letter. I realize, as I end it, that it can serve as a clarification and conclusion of that part of the discussion which concerns me.

Gratefully yours,

Antonin Artaud

ANTONIN ARTAUD TO JACQUES RIVIERE

June 6, 1924

**Dear Sir,**

.    .    .    .    .    .    .    .    .    .    .    .    .    .    .    .    .

My mental life is completely shot through with petty doubts and unarguable certainties that are expressed in lucid and coherent words. And my weaknesses are of a more trembling texture. They are themselves nebulous and ill-formulated. They have live roots, roots of anguish that reach to the heart of life. But they have not the turmoil of life. One does not feel in them the cosmic afflatus of a soul that has been shaken to its foundations. They are the weaknesses of a mind that has not pondered its weakness; if it had, it would render that weakness in dense and forceful words. And there, sir, lies the entire problem: to have within oneself the inseparable reality and material clarity of a feeling, to have them to such a degree that the feeling cannot but express itself, to have a wealth of words and formal constructions which might join in the dance, might serve one's purpose —

21

and at the very moment when the soul is about to organize its wealth, its discoveries, its revelation, at that unconscious moment when the thing is about to emanate, a higher and evil will attacks the soul like vitriol, attacks the word-and-image mass, attacks the mass of the feeling and leaves me panting as at the very door of life.

And now suppose that I feel physically the passing of this will, suppose that it shakes me with sudden, unexpected electricity, with repeated electricity. Suppose that each of my pondered instants is on certain days shaken by these deep tornadoes which are not betrayed by anything external. And tell me whether any work of literature is compatible with such states. What brain could resist them? What personality would not be dissolved in them? If only I had the strength, I would sometimes indulge myself, in thought, in the luxury of subjecting to the mortification of such pressing pain any prominent mind, any writer, young or old, who produces and whose new-born thought carries weight, in order to see what remained of him. One must not be too hasty in judging men, one must trust them to the point of absurdity, to their very dregs. These foolhardy works often seem to you the product of a mind which is not yet in possession of itself and which perhaps never will possess itself, but who knows what brain they conceal, what power of life, what mental fever which circumstances alone have reduced. Enough about myself and about my works that are still unborn. All I ask is to feel my brain.

Antonin Artaud


JACQUES RIVIERE TO ANTONIN ARTAUD

Dear M. Artaud,

Perhaps I somewhat indiscreetly substituted myself, with my ideas and prejudices, for your suffering, your singularity. Perhaps I chattered when I should have understood and pitied. I wanted to reassure you, to cure you. My line of conduct was probably due to the kind of rage with which I always react, when I myself am concerned, in the

22

direction of life. In my struggle to live, I won't admit myself beaten until I cease to breathe.

Your last letters, in which the word 'soul' frequently replaces the word 'mind,' arouse in me a sympathy that is even graver, though more embarrassed, than the first ones. I feel and touch a deep, private misery. In the presence of sufferings which I can only dimly perceive, I remain in a state of abeyance. But perhaps this puzzled attitude will be more helpful and encouraging to you than my earlier ratiocination.

And yet — am I utterly unable to understand your torments? You say that 'a man possesses himself in flashes, and even when he does possess himself he does not quite overtake himself.' That man is you. But I can also tell you that he is also I. I am not familiar with anything that resembles your 'tornadoes,' or that 'evil will' which 'attacks the soul and its powers of expression from without.' But though the feeling I sometimes have of my own inferiority may be more general, less painful, it is no less clear.

In trying to explain the alternations which I experience, I dismiss, as you do, the convenient symbol of inspiration. It is a matter of something deeper, more 'substantial,' if I may distort the meaning of this word, than a favorable wind that comes up, or does not come up, from the depths of my mind. It is a matter of degrees over which I range in my own reality. Not, alas, voluntarily, but in a purely accidental way.

What is remarkable is that the very fact of my existence is never at any moment, as you note in your own case, a matter of serious doubt for me. There always remains for me something of myself, but very often it is something poor, clumsy, feeble and almost suspect. At such moments, I do not lose all sense of my complete reality, but, at times, all hope of ever regaining it. It is like a roof above me that remains hanging in the air by some miracle and up to which I see no means of reconstructing myself.

My feelings and ideas — my usual ones — move through me with a little fantastic air; they are so weakened, so hypothetical, that they look as though they belong to a pure philosophical speculation. They are still there, nevertheless. But they look at me as if wanting to make me wonder at their absence.

Proust has described the 'intermittences of the heart'; it is the intermittences of being that should be described now.

Obviously this fading away of the soul has physiological causes that it is often rather easy to determine. You speak of soul 'as a coagulation of our nervous force'; you say that it can be 'physically affected.' I think, as you do, that it is largely dependent on the nervous system. Nevertheless, its crises are so capricious that at times I understand one's being tempted to seek, as you do, the mystical explanation of an 'evil will' eager to dwarf it from without.

In any case, it is, I think, a fact that a whole category of men are subject to shiftings of the level of being. How often do we not suddenly discover, when mechanically placing ourselves in a familiar psychological attitude, that it has transcended us, or rather that we have become surreptitiously unequal to it! How often does our most habitual personage not appear to us suddenly to be factitious and even fictive, owing to the absence of the spiritual, or 'essential,' resources that were supposed to feed it!

Where does our being go and from where does it return, that being which all psychology until our time pretended to regard as a constant? It is an almost insoluble problem, unless one have recourse to a religious dogma, like that of Grace, for example. I am amazed at the fact that our age (I am thinking of Pirandello, of Proust, in whom it is implicit) has dared raise it while leaving it in a state of a question and limiting itself to anguish.

'A soul physically affected.' That is a frightful heritage. Yet I think that in one respect, that of clearsightedness, it can also be a privilege. It is the only means we have of understanding ourselves a little, of at least seeing ourselves. He who is unfamiliar with depression, who never feels his soul being broken by the body, invaded by its weakness, is incapable of obtaining any insight into man. One must go below, must look at the underside. One must be no longer able to move, to hope, to believe, in order to perceive. How shall we distinguish our intellectual or moral mechanisms if we are not temporarily deprived of them? The consolation of those who thus experience death gradually must be the fact that they are the only ones who have some notion of how life is made up.

In addition, 'the mortification of such pressing pain' prevents the ridiculous cloud of vanity from rising up within them. You write: 'The distance that separates me from myself suffices to cure me of the judgement of others.' Such is the utility of this 'distance': it 'cures us of the judgement of others'; it prevents us from doing any thing to charm it, to adjust ourselves to it; it keeps us pure, and, despite the variations of our reality, it ensures us a higher degree of identity with ourselves.

To be sure, health is the only allowable ideal, the only one to which what I call a man has a right to aspire, but when it is given in a human being from the very beginning, it hides half the world from him.

Despite myself, I have once again let myself try to comfort you by trying to show you how precarious the 'normal state' can be even in the matter of existence. I hope with all my heart that the stages I have been describing are accessible to you in the upward direction as well as in the other. Why, after all, should a moment of plenitude, of self assurance, be forbidden you if you already have the courage to desire it. There is no absolute peril except for him who abandons himself; there is no complete death except for him who acquires a taste for dying.

With all good wishes,

Jacques Rivière

*Translated by Bernard Frechtman*

# HERE  WHERE  OTHERS . . .

Here where others offer up their works I pretend to nothing more than showing my mind.

Life is a burning up of questions.

I can't conceive of a work detached from life.

I don't love detached creation. I can no longer conceive of the mind as detached from itself. Each of my works, every one of my maps, every one of the glacial blooms of my inner soul dribbles all over me.

I recognize myself as much in a letter written to explain the intimate shrinkage of my being and the insane castration of my life, as in an essay exterior to myself that seems to me like an indifferent pregnancy of my mind.

I suffer because the Spirit is not in life and life not in the Spirit. I suffer from Spirit as organ, Spirit as translation, Spirit as intimidation-with-things, in order to make them enter into the Spirit.

I suspend this book in life, I'd like it to be bitten by external things, and first of all by all the fits and starts, all the twitching *of my future self*.

All these pages are leftover icicles of the mind. Excuse my absolute freedom. I refuse to make distinctions between any of the minutes of myself. And I don't recognize the existence of any map of the mind.

You have to do away with the mind, as with literature. I say the mind and life communicate at all levels. I want to make a Book that will derange men, that will be like an open door leading them where they would never have consented to go. A door simply ajar on reality.

And this is no more a preface to a book than the poems, for example, that stake it out, or the enumeration of all the furies of a torn soul.

This is merely an icicle stuck in my throat.

*Translated by Jack Hirschman*

# A GREAT FERVOR . . .

A great thinking and overpopulated fervor carried my being like a teeming abyss. A carnal, resonant wind blew thick with sulphurous fumes. And the tiniest of rootlets peopled this wind like a network of veins, their intersections glowing. Space was measurable, rasping, but without penetrable form. And the center of it was a mosaic of explosions, a kind of merciless cosmic hammer of a distorted heaviness, which fell again and again into the space like a forehead, but with a noise as if distilled. And the muffled enveloping of the noise had the dull urgency and penetration of a living look. Yes, the space gave out its full muffle of mind in which no thought rang clear, none able to release its discharge of things. But little by little, the mass turned like a slimy powerful nausea, a kind of immense influx of vegetal thundering blood. And the little roots trembling at the edge of my mental eye detached themselves with a dizzying speed from the mass shriveled by the wind. And the whole space trembled like a sex ransacked by the globe of burning sky. And something from the beak of an actual dove made a hole in the vague mass of states; and at that moment all profound thought stratified itself, resolved itself, became transparent and boiled down.

And now what we needed was a hand that could become the organ of apprehension itself. And two or three times more the entire vegetal mass turned, and each time my eye repositioned itself more precisely. The very obscurity became profuse and aimless. The entire gel attained complete clarity.

*Translated by Marc Estrin*


# DOCTOR —

There's a point on which I would have liked to insist: it's concerning the importance of the thing on which your injections act; this kind of essential relaxation of my being, this lowering of my mental water-level which, as one might think, doesn't mean any diminution whatever of my morality (my moral soul) or even of my intelligence but, if you wish, only of my usable intellect, of my possibilities for thought, and which has more to do with the feeling I have of myself than with what I show to others.

This hushed and multiform crystallization of thought, which chooses its form at a *given moment*. There's an immediate and direct crystallization of the self in the midst of all possible forms, all modes of thought.

And now, Monsieur le Docteur, since you are quite aware of what in me is capable of being attacked (and healed by drugs), of the litigious point of my life, I hope you have the know-how to give me the quantity of subtle liquids, of specious agents, of mental morphine which will uplift my abasement, balance what is crumbling, reunite what is separated, recompose what is destroyed.

My thought salutes you.

*Translated by David Ossman*

# DESCRIPTION OF A PHYSICAL STATE

Corrosive sensation in the limbs,

muscles as if twisted, then laid open; brittle feeling of being made of glass; wincing and cringing at any move or sound. Unconscious incoherence of steps, of gestures, of movements. Willpower constantly inhibited in even the simplest gestures,

renunciation of simple gestures,

overwhelming and CENTRAL fatigue, sort of a dark horse fatigue running for something or other. Body motions run haywire in sort of death exhaustion, mind fatigued at simplest muscular tension like gesture of grasping — unconsciously clinging to something,

holding it together by constant will power.

A fatigue of cosmic Creation, sensation of the body being dragged on and on, feeling unbelievable fragility become splitting pain,

state of painful numbness, sort of localized numbness on skin surface which does not hinder a single motion but alters nevertheless that internal feeling in your limbs so that the mere act of standing vertical is achieved only at the price of a victorious struggle.

Localized (in all probability) on the skin surface but felt like the radical suppression of a limb, transmitting to the brain no more than images of bloody old cottons pulled out in the shape of arms and legs, images of distant and dislocated members. Sort of inward breakdown of entire nervous system.

Giddiness in motion, some kind of oblique dizziness accompanying each attempted effort, heat coagulation enclosing the whole skull area or detaching itself bit by bit, moving slabs of heat.

Painful exacerbation of the skull, bladelike pressure on the nerves, back of neck determined to suffer, temples turning into glass or marble, head stamped on by horses' hooves.

So now it is high time to speak of the disembodiment of reality, this sort of breakdown which, one should think, is applied to a self-multiplication proliferating among things and the perception of them in our mind, which is where they do belong.

This instantaneous classification of things in the brain cells and not so much in their particularly logical order but in their own sentimental affective order,

(which is no longer done):

These things have no more smell, no more sex. But their logical order is also sometimes broken precisely because they do lack this emotional smell. Words decay at the unconscious command of the brain, all words for whatever and no matter what mental operation, especially those which have to do with the most habitual and active states of mind.

*Translated by David Rattray*

# THIN BELLY . . .

Thin belly. Belly of tenuous powder, as in a photograph. At the foot of this belly, an exploded grenade.

Grenade casts a scaly halo which rises like tongues of fire, cold fire.

The circulation takes the belly and turns it inside out. But the stomach does not turn.

These veins are running with a heady blood, blood mixed with saffron and sulphur but sulphur sweetened with water.

Above this stomach the breasts are visible. And up higher and deeper but on another level of the mind there is a burning sun, and the way it looks, you would think it was a breast burning. And at the foot of the grenade, a bird.

The sun seems to be staring. But it stares as if it were staring at the sun. This stare is a cone which stands headfirst in the sun. And the air is all like some clotted music, but a vast profound music, well put together and secret and full of congealed ramifications.

And all this in a masonry of pillars, in a sort of draftsman's wash by which belly and reality are in contact.

The canvas is concave, paint laid on its stratifications. Painting is well enclosed within the limits of the canvas. It is like a closed circle, sort of a bottomless whirlpool creased down the middle. Like a mind which sees and spills itself. Incessantly belabored and *remalaxified* by the nervous hand of the mind. And yet the mind sows its phosphorescence.

The mind is safe. It really does have one foot in this world. The grenade, the stomach and the breasts are all, so to speak, testimonials of reality. So are the dead bird and the multiple foliage of pillars. The air is full of pencil strokes like razor strokes or the etching of a magic fingernail.

The air has been stirred up enough.

So now it sets itself out in cells where the seeds of unreality take root. These cells are laid out fanwise in places where they belong,

around the belly, ahead of the sun, beyond the bird of liquid sulphur.

But architecture is indifferent to cells, it feeds but will not speak.

Each cell contains one egg. What germ glows in this egg? In each cell one egg is suddenly born. In each there is a kind of inhuman but limpid teeming like stratified levels of an arrested universe.

Each cell carries its egg nicely and proposes it to us, but it makes no difference to the egg whether it gets chosen or rejected.

Not all cells carry an egg. In some a screw is born. And in the air a larger screw hangs down as if it were already sulphur or phosphorus in its sheath of unreality. And this screw has all the importance the most momentous thoughts ever have.

This belly evokes surgery and the Morgue, the factory, the public place, the operating table. The body of the stomach seems to be granite or marble or plaster, but hardened plaster. A cell is therefore a mountain. And the spray of the sky a ring, pellucid and cool, around the mountain peak. The air rings clear on the mountain, pious, legendary, forbidden. Access to the mountain is forbidden. The mountain does, certainly, have its place in the soul. It is the horizon of a certain something which never stops receding. The feeling it gives is that of an ' eternal horizon.'

As for myself, I described this painting with tears in my eyes, for this painting touches my heart. I feel my thoughts radiate in it as in an ideal absolute space, except this space could really be brought into reality. And in it, I fall out of the sky.

And every fiber in me is unravelled and finds its place revealed in the predestined cells. In it, I return upwards, to my source; in it, I sense the place and position of my mind. He who painted this picture is the greatest painter in the world. To André Masson, who deserves it.

*Translated by David Rattray*


# THERE'S AN ANGUISH . . .

There's an acid and turbid anguish — powerful as a knife — whose quartering is heavy as earth; an anguish of lightning, punctuated by abysms, serried and pressed like bedbugs, like a kind of brittle vermin whose every movement is congealed; an anguish where the mind chokes and cuts itself — and kills itself.

It consumes only what belongs to it, it is born of its own asphyxiation.

31

It is a *congealing* of the marrow, an absence of mental fire, a lack of circulation of life.

But the opium anguish has another color. It doesn't have this metaphysical slant, this marvelous imperfection of accent. I imagine it full of echoes, caves, labyrinths, detours; full of talking tongues of fire, of mental eyes in action, and of somber thunderclaps bulging with reason.

But I imagine the soul as being well centered and yet divisible to infinity, and transportable as a *thing that exists*. I imagine it as a feeling mind which struggles and consents at the same time, and turns its tongues in all directions, multiplies its sex — and kills itself.

You have to know the true cutting void, the void that no longer has organs. The void of opium has something of the form of the brow of the thinker who has located the area of the black hole.

I myself speak of the absence of hole, of a kind of cold suffering without images, without feeling, like the indescribable shock of abortions.

*Translated by Jack Hirschman*

# I REALLY FELT . . .

I really felt that you were shattering the atmosphere around me, that you were creating a void in order to allow me to progress, in order to offer the expanse for an impossible space to that which within me was potentiality only, to a whole virtual germination that must be sucked into life by the interval which offered itself.

Often I placed myself in this state of impossible absurdity in order to try and generate thought inside myself. There are a few of us, in this era, who attempted to attack things, to create within ourselves the intervals for life, which didn't exist and moreover didn't seem ever to belong in space.

I have always been struck by the obstinacy of the mind in insisting on thinking in terms of dimensions and intervals, in adhering to arbitrary states of things in order to think, in thinking in segments, in crystalloids, in thinking that every mode of being solidifies at a starting-point, that thought not be in instant and uninterrupted contact with things, but that this fixation and this immobilization, this kind of erection of the soul into monuments, arises into being, so to speak, BEFORE THOUGHT. This is obviously the ideal condition for creativity.

But I am struck still more by that unrelenting, that meteoric illusion which instills in us these finite, planned and predetermined architectures, these crystallized segments of the soul, as if they were a huge malleable sheet in osmosis with all the rest of reality. And surreality is like a contraction of osmosis, a kind of communication turned inside-out. Far from a weakening of control, I see here on the contrary a far greater control, but one which instead of acting remains on guard, a control which blocks contact with commonplace reality and allows these more subtle and rarified contacts, bared down to the thread which ignites and yet never breaks apart.

I envision a well-worked soul, brimstoned and phosphorized by these contacts, as the only acceptable state of reality.

Yet it is I know not what unknown and unnameable lucidity that permits me to capture their tone and volume and compels me to feel them myself. I can feel them because of a certain insoluble totality, I mean the feeling of this cannot be questioned. And I myself, in relation to these disturbing contacts, feel in a state of incipient tremor. I would have you bring to mind a void brought to a standstill, a mass of mind buried somewhere, having become virtuality.

*Translated by Jean Decock*

# AN ACTOR YOU CAN SEE . . .

An actor you can see through crystal.
Inspiration on different levels.
Literature should not show through.
I have only aimed at the clockmaking of the soul, I've only transcribed the pain of botched adjustment.
I'm a complete abyss. Those who believe me capable of a total sor-

row, of a beautiful sorrow, of full and fleshy anguishes, of anguishes
that are a mixture of objects, an excited manipulation of powers and
not a suspended point
    — with nevertheless animated uprooting impulses
    which come from the confrontation of my forces
    with these abysms of proffered absolute
    (from the confrontation of forces of powerful size)
    and all that is left are the voluminous abysms, the
    stopwork, the cold —
those who've attributed me with more life, judged me to be less far
gone, believed I'd been plunged into an excruciating noise, into a vio-
lent blackness with which I was struggling
    are lost in the darkness of man.

In sleep, nerves taut the length of the legs.

Sleep came from being out of step with my belief, I was losing my
grip and the absurd was stepping on my toes.

You have to understand that all intelligence is only a vast eventual-
ity, and that you can lose it, not like the lunatic who's dead but like a
being in the midst of life who feels its attraction and its breath (of in-
telligence, not of life).

Titillations of the intelligence and this brusque reversal of parts.
Words halfway to intelligence.

This possibility of thinking backwards and suddenly insulting one's
thought.

This dialogue within thought.

The absorption, the rupture of everything.

And all at once this trickle of water on a volcano, the thin fall and
slowing down of the mind.

Finding oneself again in a state of extreme shock, enlightened by
unreality, with fragments of the real world in a corner of one's self.

To think without minimum rupture, without a trap in the thought,
without any one of these sudden magic tricks to which my marrow is
accustomed, like transmitters of currents.

My marrow sometimes has fun with, takes pleasure in these games, is pleased with these furtive abductions at which the head of my thought presides.

All I need sometimes is a single word, one simple little word, without importance, to be great, to speak in the tone of the prophets: a word-witness, a precise word, a subtle word, a word well-soaked in my marrow, gone out of me and standing at the extreme limit of my being, a word which, for everybody, would be nothing.

I am witness, I am the only witness of myself. This crust of words — these imperceptible transformations of my thought in whispers, this small part of my thought which I claim had already been formulated and which has miscarried, —

I am the only judge in measuring its scope.

A kind of constant waste of the normal standard of reality.

Under this crust of bone and skin which is my head, there is a constant anguish — not like a moral point, or the ratiocinations of an imbecilically fastidious nature, or inhabited by a leaven of worries in the sense of height, but like a decantation

inside,

like the dispossessing of my vital substance,

like the physical and essential loss

(I mean loss from the standpoint of the essence)

of sense.

Impotence to crystallize unconsciously the broken point of automatism to any degree whatsoever.

The difficulty really is in finding one's place and rediscovering communication with one's self. Everything lies in a certain flocculation of things, in an assortment of all these mental stones around a point which is precisely what we are searching for.

And here is what I, Artaud, think of thought:

INSPIRATION DOES EXIST.

And there is a phosphorescent point where all reality is rediscovered, but changed, metamorphosed — and by what? — a point open for the *magic* usage of things. And I believe in mental meteors, in individual cosmogonies.

Do you know what suspended sensitivity is, this frightening vitality schismed in two. This point of necessary cohesion where being no longer rises. This menacing, this overwhelming place.

Translated by David Ossman

## HERE IS SOMEONE . . .

Here is someone in whose mind no place crystallizes, someone who can't all of a sudden feel his soul on his left side, the heart-side. Here is someone for whom life is a fixed point, someone for whom the soul has no sides nor the spirit any beginnings.

I'm an imbecile because of the suppression of thought, the malformation of thought. I'm empty because of the stupefaction of my tongue.

Malformation, mal-agglomeration of a certain number of these vittreous corpuscles you make such prodigal use of. A use you know nothing about, having never watched it.

All the terms I choose to think with are for me really *TERMS* in the proper sense of the word — veritable terminations limiting the boundaries of my mental [      ], of all the states I've exposed my thought to. I'm truly LOCALIZED by my terms, and if I say I am LOCALIZED by my terms it's because I don't regard them as valid in my thought. I'm completely paralyzed by my terms, by a chain of terminations. And regardless of WHERE my thoughts may be at these moments, I can only get them out through these terms — however contradictory, or parallel, or equivocal they may be — or else I have to stop thinking.

If one could only take pleasure in one's own Void, if one could settle down in his own Void, and if this Void were neither a certain kind of being nor also completely a death.

It's so hard to no longer exist, to no longer BE, as part of something. The real pain is to feel thought shifting inside you. But thought, like a point, is not definitely a pain.

I'm at the point where I no longer touch life, yet I have inside me all the appetites and insistent titillations of being. And am concerned with only one thing: making myself over.

There's no correlation for me between words and the exact states of my being.

' But this is normal, everyone lacks the right word, you're too hard on yourself, to listen to you it wouldn't seem . ., you express yourself perfectly in French, you attach too much importance to words.'

You're all asses, intelligent skinny perceptive or tough, you're all asses, I mean you're dogs, I mean you go around barking, you rabidly persist in not understanding. I know myself and that's enough for me. It has to be enough. I know myself because I'm there, I'm there at Antonin Artaud.

— You may know yourself, but we see you. We see clearly what you're doing.

— Yes, but you don't see what I'm thinking.

At each stage of my thinking machine there are gaps, traps.

Please understand me, I don't mean in time, I mean in a certain kind of space (I see what I mean); I don't mean a thought lengthwise, a thought having the time-dimension of thoughts; I mean one thought, a thought by itself, but a thought FROM INSIDE; but I don't mean a thought by Pascal, a philosopher's thought; I mean a twisted fixation, a sclerosis of a specific state. Catch that!

I study myself microscopically. I put my finger on the exact place of the fault, the unadmitted sliding. For the mind is more reptilian than even you, Gentlemen. It slips away like snakes, it slips away until it affects our tongues, I mean it leaves them hanging.

I'm the man who's best felt the astounding disorder of his language in its relation to his thought. I am the man who has best charted his inmost self, his most imperceptible slitherings. Really, I lose myself in my thought the way one dreams, the way one suddenly returns to his thought. I am the man who knows the innermost recesses of loss.

*Translated by Marc Estrin*

# ALL WRITING IS PIGSHIT . . .

All writing is pigshit.

People who leave the obscure and try to define whatever it is that goes on in their heads, are pigs.

The whole literary scene is a pigpen, especially this one.

All those who have vantage points in their spirit, I mean, on some side or other of their heads and in a few strictly localized brain areas; all those who are masters of their language; all those for whom words have a meaning; all those for whom there exist sublimities in the soul and currents of thought; all those who are the spirit of the times, and have named these currents of thought — and I am thinking of their precise works, of that automatic grinding that delivers their spirit to the winds —

are pigs.

Those for whom certain words have a meaning, and certain manners of being; those who are so fussy; those for whom emotions are classifiable, and who quibble over some degree or other of their hilarious classifications; those who still believe in 'terms'; those who brandish whatever ideologies belong to the hierarchy of the times; those about whom women talk so well, and also those women who talk so well, who talk of the contemporary currents of thought; those who still believe in some orientation of the spirit; those who follow paths, who drop names, who fill books with screaming headlines

are the worst kind of pigs.

And you are quite aimless, young man!

No, I am thinking of bearded critics.

And I told you so: no works of art, no language, no word, no thought, nothing.

Nothing; unless maybe a fine Brain-Storm.

A sort of incomprehensible and totally erect stance in the midst of everything in the mind.

And don't expect me to tell you what all this is called, and how many parts it can be divided into; don't expect me to tell you its weight; or to get back in step and start discussing all this so that by discussing I may get lost myself and even, without even realizing it, start THINKING. And don't expect this thing to be illuminated and live and deck itself out in a multitude of words, all neatly polished as to meaning, very diverse, and capable of throwing light on all the attitudes and all the nuances of a very sensitive and penetrating mind.

Ah, these states which have no name, these sublime situations of the soul, ah these intervals of wit, these minuscule failures which are the daily bread of my hours, these people swarming with data . . . they are always the same old words I'm using, and really I don't seem to make much headway in my thoughts, but I am really making more headway than you, you beard-asses, you pertinent pigs, you masters of fake verbiage, confectioners of portraits, pamphleteers, ground-floor lace-curtain herb collectors, entomologists, plague of my tongue.

I told you so, I no longer have the gift of tongue. But this is no reason you should persist and stubbornly insist on opening your mouths.

Look, I will be understood ten years from now by the people who then will do what you are doing now. Then my geysers will be recognized, my glaciers will be seen, the secret of diluting my poisons will have been learnt, the plays of my soul will be deciphered.

Then all my hair, all my mental veins will have been drained in quicklime; then my bestiary will have been noticed, and my mystique become a hat. Then the joints of stones will be seen smoking, arborescent bouquets of mind's eyes will crystallize in glossaries, stone aeroliths will fall, lines will be seen and the geometry of the void understood: people will learn what the configuration of the mind is, and they will understand how I lost my mind.

They will then understand why my mind is not all here; then they will see all languages go dry, all minds parched, all tongues shrivelled up, the human face flattened out, deflated as if sucked up by shriveling leeches. And this lubricating membrane will go on floating in the air, this caustic lubricating membrane, this double membrane of multiple degrees and a million little fissures, this melancholic and vitreous membrane, but so sensitive and also pertinent, so capable of multiplying, splitting apart, turning inside out with its glistening little cracks, its dimensions, its narcotic highs, its penetrating and toxic injections, and

    all this then will be found to be all right,
    and I will have no further need to speak.

*Translated by David Rattray*

# FRAGMENTS OF A JOURNAL IN HELL

Neither my screaming nor my fever is really mine. My secondary faculties (these elements of my mind and soul are hidden) are disintegrating, but just imagine how they are hanging on.

Something halfway between the typical atmosphere I breathe and the tip of my reality.
I hunger less for food than some kind of elementary consciousness.
This knot of life where thought-emission hangs.
A knot of central suffocation.

Simply to find basis in some unambiguous truth, that is, one which would depend on one unique razor's edge.

This problem of the emaciation of my conscious being is no longer presented in its exclusively excruciating aspect. I feel new factors intervening in the process by which my life is being denatured, and that

I have something like a new awareness of my intimate loss.

I see in the fact that the die is cast and I am plunging into the affirmation of a guessed-at-truth, however risky, my entire reason for being alive. Sometimes I linger for hours over the impression some idea or sound has made on me. My emotion does not develop in time, it has no temporal sequence at all. The ebb and flow of my soul are in perfect accord with the absolute ideality of mind.

To confront the metaphysical system I made for myself as a consequence of this void I carry within me.

From this pain rooted in me like a wedge, at the center of my purest reality, at the point of my sensibility where the two worlds of body and mind are joined, I learn to distract myself by the effect of a false suggestion.

For in the space of that minute the illumination of a lie can last, I manufacture a notion of escape; I rush off in any wrong direction my blood takes. I close the eyes of my intelligence and open my mouth to the speech of the unspoken; I give myself the illusion of a system whose vocabulary escapes me. But from this minute of error there remains the feeling that I have snatched something real from the unknown. I believe in spontaneous bewitchments. It is impossible that I shall not some day discover a truth somewhere on the routes my blood carries me.

Paralysis is gaining, so I am less and less able to turn about. I no longer have any support, any base . . . I search for myself I don't know where. My mind is no longer able to go in the directions my emotions and the fantasies welling up in me send it. I feel castrated even in my slightest impulses. I am finally able to see the light through myself only by means of an utter renunciation of my intelligence and feeling. It must be understood that it is the living man in me who is affected, and that this paralysis stifling me is at the center — not of my feeling I am a predestined man, but of my usual personality. I am definitely set apart from life. My torment is as subtle and refined as it is harsh. It costs me mad efforts of imagination, increased tenfold by the grip of this stifling asphyxia, to succeed in *thinking* my ills. And if I keep on and persevere in this pursuit, in this need to fix once and for all the state of my suffocation . . .

You were wrong to mention this paralysis that threatens me. It really is threatening and gaining on me every day. It already exists, and like a horrible reality. Certainly I still (but for how long?) do as I please with the limbs of my body, but it has been a long time since I had any control over my mind and so my unconscious controls me altogether, by impulses coming up from my nervous rages and the tornado of my blood. Hurried and rapid images which speak to me only in words of anger and blind hate but are over as fast as a knife stabbing, or lightning in congested sky.

I am stigmatized by an urgent death, so that actual death holds no terrors for me.

I have a feeling the despair these dreadful forms advancing on me bring with them is alive. It slips into this life-knot beyond which the routes of eternity extend. It is really eternal separation. They slip their knife into this center where I feel myself human; they sever the vital connections by which I am joined to the dream of my lucid reality.

Forms of a capital despair (really essential)
Crossroads of separations,
Crossroad of the awareness of my flesh,
Abandoned by my body,
Abandoned by every possible human feeling.
I cannot compare it to anything but that state known at the heart
of delirium during a grave illness.

It is this contradiction between my inner facility and my external
difficulty which creates the torment I am dying of.

Let time march on and the social convulsions of the world ravage
the thoughts of men, I am still immune from all thought immersed in
phenomena. Just leave me to my extinguished clouds, my immortal
impotence, my unreasonable hopes. But I want it understood that I will
not abdicate a single one of my errors. If I used poor judgement, my
flesh was at fault; but these illuminations my mind allows to filter
through hour after hour are my flesh, whose blood is sheathed in light-
ning.

He speaks to me of Narcissism and my answer to him is, we are
speaking about my life. This is no ego but the cult of flesh, with the
whole weight and substance of this word Flesh. Things do not move
me except as they affect my flesh and coincide with it at the exact point
where they stir it, and not beyond that point. Nothing moves me or
interests me except what addresses itself *directly* to my body. And now
he speaks to me about the Self. My answer to him is the Ego and the
Self are two distinct terms and not to be confused; in fact, it is pre-
cisely this pair of determinants which, balancing each other, maintain
the body's equilibrium.

I can feel the ground slipping out from under my thought, and I am forced to contemplate these terms I use, unsupported by their intimate meaning or personal substratum in me. Even better than that, the point whereby this substratum seems to connect with my life becomes all of a sudden strangely tangible and virtual for me. I am struck by the idea of an unexpected and fixed space where normally all is movements, communication, interferences, trajectory.

But this erosion which subverts the very basis of my thought in its most urgent communications with the intelligence and the instinctual parts of the mind does not take place in the domain of an intangible abstraction, where only higher faculties of the intellect would participate. More than the mind which holds together, bristling with points, it is the nervous trajectory of thought which this erosion subverts and perverts. It is in the limbs and the blood that this absence and this standstill are especially felt.

A terrible cold,
An atrocious abstinence,
The limbo of a nightmare of bone and muscles, with the sensation of stomach functions snapping like a flag in the phosphorescences of the storm.
Larval images that are pushed as if by a finger and have no relation to any material thing.

I am human by my hands and my feet, my guts, my meat heart, my stomach whose knots fasten me to the rot of life.

They speak to me of words but this thing has nothing to do with words; it is a question of the mind's duration.

44

It should not be imagined that the soul has nothing to do with this bark of words peeling off. Life is there, alongside the mind, and the human being is inside the circle this mind turns on, and joined to it by a multitude of fibers . . .

No, all the physical rendings, all the diminutions of physical activity and this vexation at feeling dependent on one's body, and this body itself weighed down with marble and resting on a poor support, do not equal the anguish which comes from being deprived of physical know-ledge and the sense of one's own interior balance. When the soul lacks a language or language a mind, and the rupture ploughs a vast furrow of despair and blood in the sensory field, this is the greatest pain: for it subverts not merely the bark or the skeleton, but the very STUFF of the body. In losing this erratic spark which one felt WAS, there is this abyss consuming the entire field of the possible universe, and this feeling of uselessness that is like the knot of death. This uselessness is like the moral tone of this abyss and of its intense stupefaction, and the physical color of it is the taste of blood spurting in cascades from the orifices of the skull.

There is no use telling me this cutthroat is inside me: I am part of life, I represent the destiny that elects me, and it is impossible that all earthly life would count me in with it at a given moment, for by its very nature it threatens the life-principle.

There is a certain thing above all human activity: it is the example of this monotonous crucifixion, this crucifixion wherein the soul is for-ever being lost.

The cord which connects my intelligence, which preoccupies me,

45

with the unconscious, which feeds me, reveals more and more subtle fibers at the heart of its tree-like tissue. And it is a new life being born, a life which is more and more profound, eloquent, deep rooted.

Nothing precise can ever be reported by this soul which is strangling itself, for the torment which kills it, flays it fiber by fiber, takes place below the mind's threshold, below the threshold of what language can say; since the very connection (of what constitutes this soul and keeps it mentally together) is getting torn open little by little as life calls it toward unbroken lucidity. And there will never be lucidity concerning this passion, this kind of cyclical and fundamental matyrdom. And yet it does live, but its duration is here and there eclipsed, the fleeting keeps mingling with the fixed, and chaos with this incisive language of a lucidity without duration. This curse could be highly instructive for the depths it fills, but this world will never learn.

The emotion brought about by the blooming of a form, the adaptation of my body fluids to the virtuality of a discourse of no duration at all is a state much more precious to me than the gratification of my activity.

It is the touchstone of certain spiritual lies.

This sort of backward step the mind takes when consciousness stares it in the face, to search for the emotion of being alive. That emotion, situated outside the particular spot where the mind looked for it, and emerging with its density rich in forms and freshly flowing; that emotion which gives the overwhelming sound of matter to the spirit, the entire soul passing into its ardent fire. But what delights the soul even more than fire is the limpidity, the facility, the natural and glacial candor of this too fresh matter which breathes both hot and cold.

He is the one who knows what the appearance of this matter signifies and what underground massacre was the price of its unfolding. This material is the standard of a nothingness, which does not know itself.

When I think of myself, my thought seeks itself in the ether of a new dimension. I am on the moon as others are sitting at their balcony. I am part of the gravitation of the planets in the fissures of my mind.

Life will perpetuate itself, events will go on happening, spiritual conflicts will be resolved, and I will play no part in them. I have nothing to hope for on either side, moral or physical. For me there is perpetual sorrow and shadow, the night of the soul, and I have no voice to cry out.

Cast your riches far from this numb body, for it is insensible to the seasons of the spirit or the flesh.

I have chosen the domain of sorrow and shadow as others have chosen that of the glow and the accumulation of things.

I do not labor within the scope of any domain.

My only labor is in eternity itself.

*Translated by David Rattray*

# WHO, IN THE HEART . . .

Who, in the heart of certain anxieties at the bottom of some dreams, has not known death as a shattering and miraculous sensation with which nothing in the order of mental experience could ever be confused? You have to have experienced this gasping crescendo of anguish which comes over you in waves, and then swells you as if blown up by some unbearable bellows. The anguish draws nigh and then withdraws, but each time fuller, each time more ponderous and apoplectic. Which the body itself is, having reached its limits of distension and force — and yet it must go on. It is a sort of suction-cup on the soul whose tartness is like an acid slurping up the limits of what is feelable. And the soul cannot even fall back on a breakdown. For this distension itself is false. Death is not so easily satisfied. This distension, in the order of physical experience, is like a film negative of that shrinking process which is to keep the mind busy *over the entire area of the living body.*

This held-in gasp is the last, really the last. It is time for taking stock. The minute feared so much, dreaded so much and so much dreamt of is here. And it is true that one is going to die. One watches and measures his breath. And time unfurls completely, in all its immensity, and is resolved in such a way that it is bound to dissolve without a trace.

Go ahead and die, you poor dogged bone. They are quite aware that your thought is not complete or finished; in fact no matter which way you turn your head, you haven't even *started* thinking.

Which makes no difference. The fear you are assailed by now is drawing and quartering you in exact proportion to this impossibility. For you are quite aware that you have to make it to this other side which nothing in you, not even this body — above all, this body you will take leave of without ever forgetting its substance, thickness, and impossible asphyxia — is prepared for.

And indeed it will be like a bad dream, where you are outside the bearings of the body which you still managed to drag this far, making you suffer and being enlightened by its deafening impressions; where the perspective is always bigger or smaller than you; where nothing in the feeling you bring to it of an archetypical ground orientation can any longer be satisfied.

So that's it, and that's where it's always at. And what howl like a dog barking in a dream in the feeling of this desolation and malaise without name makes your flesh crawl, and you gag in the panic of a mad drowning: No, it isn't so. It is not so.

But the worst thing about it is, it is so. And at the same time you get this feeling of desperate truth, where it seems you are going to die again, you are going to die a second time (You say it to yourself, you open your mouth and say it, you are going to die. You are going to die *I am going to die a second time*) — just at that very moment some humidity, a moistness from iron or rock or wind, refreshes you unbelievably and consoles your thought, and you yourself liquefy as you flow to your death, to your new state of death. This running water is death; and from the moment you contemplate yourself serenely and record your new sensations, the great identification begins. You died, and yet here you are again, living — EXCEPT THIS TIME YOU ARE ALONE.

I have just described a sensation of anguish and dream, the anguish seeping into your dreams, and this is more or less how I imagine agony seeps into you and perfects itself finally in death.

Anyhow, such dreams cannot lie. And they do not lie. And these death sensations laid out end to end, this suffocation, this despair, these spells of drowsiness, this desolation, this silence — don't we see them in the enlarged suspension of a dream, with the feeling that one of the faces of a new reality is perpetually looking over our shoulder?

But the bottom of death or dream is where anguish really takes hold. This anguish, like a rubber-band stretched then suddenly snapping in your throat, is neither unknown nor novel. The death you seeped into unawares, your body turning back into a clot, this skull — it had to pass through, bearer of consciousness and life, and consequently of supreme suffocation, and consequently of superior dismemberment — it, too, had to pass through the smallest possible opening. But it agonizes to the limit of the pores; and this skull, by dint of shaking and turning fearfully, has got the idea, the feeling, that it is swollen up and its terror has assumed a shape full of pimples underneath the skin.

And so, after all, there is nothing new about death, but on the contrary it is all too well-known; for, at the end of this distillation of the viscera, don't we see the image of a panic we have already felt more than once? The very force of despair lies in that it is a seeming restitution of certain childhood situations when death appeared in such clarity, like a gush of continual disruption. Childhood knows sudden awakenings of the mind, intense prolongations of thought which get lost again at a later age. In certain childhood panics, in certain grandiose and irrational fears in which lurks the feeling of an extra-human threat, the incontestable fact is that death appears

like the rending of a nearby membrane, like the lifting of a veil which is the world — amorphous, badly shored-up as ever.

Who has no memory of unimaginable magnifications on the order of a total mental reality, and which were not at all amazing at the time, but were given, truly delivered, to the forest of one's childhood perceptions? These mental prolongations were impregnated with perfect knowledge, impregnated all things, were crystallized, eternal.

But what strange thoughts it emphasizes, from what disintegrated meteor it reconstitutes the human atoms.

The child sees recognizable throngs of ancestors in which he notes the origins of all known man-to-man resemblances. The world of appearances swells and overflows into the impalpable and the unknown. But an overshadowing of life occurs, and henceforth such states will not recur unless graced with a lucidity which is totally abnormal and due, for example, to narcotics.

Hence the immense utility of these poisons to liberate and heighten the mind. True or false from the standpoint of a reality we have seen we could set small store by, this reality being only one of the most transitory and least recognizable faces of infinite reality, this reality being the same as matter and decaying with it, narcotics regain from the mental standpoint their superior dignity, which makes them the closest and most useful helpers of death.[1]

This straitjacket death where the soul writhes in trying to regain at last a complete and permeable state,

where everything would not be shock nor the jagged edges of a delirious confusion of rationalizations without end, mingling in the fibres of a simultaneously unbearable and melodious synthesis,

where everything would not feel sick,

where the smallest place would not be incessantly reserved for the greatest hunger, the hunger for an absolute space that would be definitive this time,

where under this paroxysmal pressure there suddenly would break through the feeling of a new level,

where from the bottom of a nameless synthesis this writhing, snort-

---

[1] I affirm, and will not let go of the idea, that death is not outside the field of the mind, and that it is, within certain limitations, recognizable and approachable by a certain sensibility.

Everything in the order of the written word which abandons the field of ordered and lucid perceptions; everything which aims at creating a reversal of appearances, to introduce doubt about the position of mental images and their relationship; everything which provokes confusion without weakening the burst of mental energy; everything which disrupts the relationships of things while giving this agitated mental energy an even greater aspect of truth and violence — all these offer death an exit, and relate us to certain most subtle states of the mind, at the heart of which death wants out.

This is why all who dream without regretting their dreams, without bringing back from the plunge into a fertile unconscious this feeling of an atrocious nostalgia, are pigs. The dream is true. All dreams are true. I have a feeling of harshness, of landscapes as if sculpted, of swaying patches of ground covered over with a sort of cool sand, and they mean:

'Regret, disappointment, abandonment, separation, when will we meet again?'

Nothing so resembles love as the appeal of certain dream landscapes, the encirclement of certain hills by a clay-like material whose forms seem molded on our thoughts.

When will we meet again? When will the earthy taste of your lips again touch my anxious spirit? Earth is like some kind of whirlwind of mortal lips. Life scoops up ahead of us the pit of all the caresses that somehow we missed. What can we do with this angel at our side, whose apparition never happened? Will all our sensations be forever intellectual, and will our dreams never succeed in kindling a soul whose feelings will help us die? What is this death we are alone in forever, where love never teaches us the way?

ing soul might feel the possibility as in dreams of waking up in a more lucid world after having perforated it knows not what barrier — and finds itself in a luminosity where at last its limbs relax, in a place where all worldly partitions seem infinitely fragile.

This soul could be reborn; however, it is not reborn. For although eased somewhat, it feels it is still dreaming, it hasn't yet transformed itself into that dream state with which it cannot yet fully identify.

At this instant of his mortal daydream, the living man come to the great wall of an impossible identification brutally withdraws his soul.

There he is, cast out and onto the naked level of the senses, in a light without dimension.

Outside the infinite musicality of his nerve waves, prey to the boundless hunger of the air, to the absolute cold.

*Translated by David Rattray*

# TRANSPARENT ABELARD

Humming, the armature of the sky continues to trace on the window pane of his soul the same amorous signs, the same warm communications, which would perhaps be able to save him from being a man if only he would consent to save himself from love.

He must give in. He can't contain himself any longer. He gives up. That melodic seething pressing him. His penis pulses: a tormenting wind murmurs, making a sound higher than heaven. The river flows with female corpses. Ophelia? Beatrice? Laura? No, ink, no, wind, no reeds, river-banks, shores, foam, snowflakes. The floodgates are down. Out of his own desire Abelard has made himself a floodgate. To the confluence of the atrocious and melodic surge. And it's Heloise tumbling, carried, to him — AND SHE IS WILLING.

Up there in the sky, the hand of Erasmus sows the bitter seeds of madness. Ah, what a curious germination. The Great Bear's wanderings fix time in the sky and the sky in Time, from that reversed side of the earth where the sky offers her face. An immense releveling.

It's because heaven has a face that Abelard has a heart in which so many stars supremely sprout up and whip his tail. Behind all the metaphysics is his love, all paved in flesh, glowing with stones, born in the sky after so many many sowings of the seeds of madness.

But Abelard swats away heaven like a blue-tail fly. Strange defeat. How to get away? God! Quick, the eye of a needle! The smallest needle's eye, so that Abelard won't be able to come looking for us.

The day is strangely beautiful. From now on it can't be otherwise. For as of today Abelard no longer is chaste. The tight chain of books is broken. He renounces the chaste coitus permitted by God.

How beautiful the act of love is! Even when human, even while enjoying the body of a woman, what seraphic and intimate voluptuousness. Heaven within reach of earth, and less beautiful. Paradise embedded in his nails.

For the call of heavenly lightning, even from the tower's top, can't compare with the span of a woman's thighs. Isn't this Abelard the priest for whom love is so clear?

How clear the love act, how clear the sin. So clear. What seeds, how sweet these flowers are to the swooning sex, how voracious the heads of pleasure, how pleasure spreads her poppies to the extremes of the game. Her poppies of sound, of daylight and music, swiftly, like a magnetic tearing of birds. Pleasure playing a trenchant and mystic melody on the sharp edge of a thin dream. Oh! that dream where love consents to open its eyes once more! Yes, Heloise, it's me who strides in you with all my philosophy, it's me who abandons within you all ornaments and gives you instead the men whose spirit trembles and glistens inside you. — Let Spirit marvel at itself, since at last Woman marvels at Abelard. Let the foam spring at the deep and glowing walls. The trees. Attila's vegetation.

He has her. He possesses her. She smothers him. And each page loosens its bow and advances. This book in which the pages of the brain are turned.

Abelard's cut his hands. But from now on, what symphony is equal to that atrocious kiss of paper? Heloise swallows fire. Opens a door. Climbs the stairs. A bell. Her sweet, crushed breasts rise up. Her skin is even whiter on her breasts. Her body is white, but blemished, for no woman's belly is pure. Their skins are the color of mildew. Their belly smells good, but how poor it is. And so many generations dream of this one. And here it is. Abelard, a man, holds it. Glorious belly. That's it, and yet it isn't. Eat straw and fire. The kiss opens its caverns where the sea comes to die. There it is, the spasm, with heaven concurring, toward which a spiritual coalition unfurls, AND IT COMES FROM ME. Ah, I feel as if I were nothing but guts, without the bridge of the spirit above me. Without so many magical meanings, so many additional secrets. She and I. We're really there. I'm holding her. I'm kissing her. One last pressure holds me back, freezes me. I feel the Church, between my thighs, moaning, holding on to me. Will it paralyze me? Will I pull out? No, no! I'm smashing the last wall. Saint Francis of Assisi, ex-guardian of my sex, draws aside. Sainte Brigitte unclenches my teeth. Saint Augustine undoes my belt. Sainte Catherine of Siena puts God to sleep. It's over, oh it's over, I'm no longer a virgin. The heavenly wall has turned around. Universal madness is catching up with me. I scale my delight to the highest ethereal summits.

But now Sainte Heloise hears him. Later, infinitely later, she hears and speaks to him. A kind of night fills his teeth. Enters, roaring into the caverns of his skull. With her insect-spindly hands she nudges open the lid of his tomb. You might think you heard a goat in a dream. She's trembling, but he's trembling far worse than she. Poor man! Poor Antonin Artaud! For it's really him, this impotent wretch sealing the stars, trying to confront his weakness with the cardinal points of the elements, endeavoring to compose from each of the subtle or solidified faces of nature one thought that will hold together, one image that will stand. If only he could create as many elements, furnish at least the metaphysics of disaster, the beginning would be the downfall!

Heloise regrets that she didn't have, in place of her womb, a wall like the one she leaned against when Abelard pricked her with his obscene sting. For Artaud, privation is the beginning of the death he desires. What a beautiful image: a eunuch!

*Translated by Marc Estrin*

# IN THE LIGHT OF THE EVIDENCE . . .

In the light of the evidence and of the reality of the brain,
at a point where we are able to get the sound and feel of things in
this world,
with the eyes of a man who is dependent and feels things building
up again in him and fixes on the start of a new reality.

Those states where the simplest most commonplace reality does not
reach me, where the instant pressure of habitual reality never gets
through to me, where I don't even reach the level of bare subsistance.

Then let this pressure and this feeling you've got inside get out in
the light of day and expose their obvious side and their normal density
to the world, which figures with what you represent in a system, with
an amount representing you, with *the amount* that represents you.

Not, strictly speaking, just the bulk of things, but also their feel and
resonance in me: the resonance which results in thought.

To get carried away by things instead of fixing on some of their
more specious sides, and always to be looking for definitions which re-
veal only the smallest aspects of the thing,

but still to have in oneself the current of things, to be level with
that current and at least to be level with life instead of always being
left in the interval by our deplorable mental condition,

to be level with objects and things, having both their global shape
and their definition at once inside you,

and have the focal points of gray matter start their motion every
time their feel and vision of them inside you starts moving.
*

Once and for all
(a) it really seems I am dead-set on demonstrating that I do not
think and realize it and I am feeble minded but I think all humans
are feeble minded and, secondly, it is better to be feeble and in a per-
petual state of abdication towards your mind. It is a better state for
man, it is a more normal state, better adapted to our sinister human
state, to this sinister pretence of men to will.

I have a stupefied imagination.

*

We are hemmed in on all sides by mountains of problems:
Damn anyone who thinks he could escape them, damn him if he
thought he could do without thinking.

What period in history contains and can show as an asset this des-
perate attempt to conquer, which takes place on the icy summits of
the Mind.

*Translated by David Rattray*

## ON SUICIDE

Before committing suicide, I ask that I be given some real assurance
of being; I should like to be sure about death. To me, life seems
merely like a consent to the apparent legibility of things and their co-
herence in the mind. I no longer feel like some irreducible crossroad
of things death heals, heals by severing us from nature; yet what if I
am no longer anything but a mere detour ridden by pains but not by
things?

If I commit suicide, it will not be to destroy myself but to put my-
self back together again. Suicide will be for me only one means of vio-
lently reconquering myself, of brutally invading my being, of anticipat-
ing the unpredictable approaches of God. By suicide, I reintroduce my
design in nature, I shall for the first time give things the shape of my
will. I free myself from the conditioned reflexes of my organs, which
are so badly adjusted to my inner self, and life is for me no longer an
absurd accident whereby I think what I am told to think. But now I
choose my thought and the direction of my faculties, my tendencies,
my reality. I place myself between the beautiful and the hideous, the
good and evil. I put myself in suspension, without innate propensities,
neutral, in the state of equilibrium between good and evil solicitations.

For life itself is no solution, life has no kind of existence which is
chosen, consented to, and self-determined. It is a mere series of hungers
and adverse forces, of petty contradictions which succeed or miscarry
according to the circumstances of an odious gamble. Like genius, like

56

madness, evil is unequally apportioned in each man. And as with evil, likewise with good: both are the product of circumstances and of a more or less active leavening.

Certainly, it is abject to be created and to live and feel yourself in the darkest corners of your mind, down to the most *unthought of* ramifications of your irreducibly predetermined being. After all, we are only trees and it is probably written in some crook or other of my family tree that I shall kill myself on a given day.

The very idea of the freedom of suicide falls down like a lopped tree. I create neither the time nor the place nor the circumstances of my suicide. I do not even invent the thought of it; will I at least feel it when it uproots me?

It may well be that at that very instant my being will dissolve; but what if it remains whole? How will my ruined organs react? With what impossible organs will I register the laceration of this suicide?

I feel death upon me like a torrent, like an instantaneous bound of lightning whose capacity surpasses my imagination. I feel a death loaded with pleasures, with swirling labyrinths. Where is the idea of my being therein?

But look at God all of a sudden like a fist, like a scythe of slicing light. I willingly severed myself from life, I wished to turn my destiny inside-out.

This God has disposed of me to the point of absurdity. He has kept me alive in a void of negations and furious renunciations of myself; he destroyed in me everything, down to the finest dust of conscious, sentient life.

He reduced me to being like a walking robot, but this robot felt the rupture of his unconscious self.

And how I have wished to produce proof of my life. I wish to get back in touch with the resonant reality of things, I wish to smash my pre-destination.

And what does this God say to that?

I had no feeling of life, every moral idea was like a dry arroyo in my veins. For me, life was no object or shape; it had become a series of rationalizations. But these rationalizations, like a motor running, didn't even get off the ground, but were inside me like possible ' diagrams ' which my will vainly tried to rivet on.

But even to get to this state of suicide, I must await the return of my conscious self; I must have a free hand in all the articulations of my being. God has placed me in despair as in a constellation of dead-ends, whose radiance culminates in me.

I can neither live nor die, nor am I capable of not wishing to die or live. And all mankind resembles me.

*Translated by David Rattray*

## SITUATION OF THE FLESH

I reflect on life. All the systems I may erect never will match these cries of a man engaged in remaking his life.

I conceive a system in which all of man would be involved, with his physical body and its heights, the intellectual projection of his mind.

As far as I am concerned, you have to reckon above all with man's incomprehensible magnetism, with what, for lack of a more piercing expression, I am obliged to call his life-force.

One day my reason must surely honor the undefined forces beseiging me — so that they replace higher thought —, those forces which, exteriorly, have the form of a cry. There are intellectual cries, cries which proceed from the *delicacy* of the marrow. Which I call the Flesh. I don't separate my thought from my life. With each vibration of my tongue I return over the paths of my thought to my flesh.

You have to have been deprived of life, of the nervous irradiation of existence, of the conscious fulfilment of the nerve, to become aware of the extent to which the Sensibility and Science of every thought is hidden in the nervous vitality of the marrow, and to what degree those who bank solely on Intelligence or absolute Intellectuality are in error. Above all is the essence of the nerve. Fulfillment which contains all consciousness and all the occult paths of the mind in the flesh.

But what am I in the midst of this theory of the Flesh, or rather

58

of Existence? I'm a man who has lost his life and is seeking by every means to reintegrate it in its proper place. In a way I'm the Animator of my own vitality: a vitality more precious to me than my conscience, for what to others is only the means for being a Man is for me the whole Reason.

In the course of this quest into the hidden limbo of my consciousness, I believed I felt explosions like the collision of occult stones or the sudden petrification of fires. Fires that would be like unconscious truths miraculously vitalized.

But you have to tread slowly on the road of dead stones, especially if you have lost *understanding of words*. It is an indescribable science which explodes by slow thrusts. And whoever possesses it doesn't understand it. But the Angels also do not understand, for all true knowledge is obscure. Clear mind belongs to matter, I mean the mind clear at a given moment.

But I have to examine this aspect of the flesh that should provide me with a metaphysic of Being and the definitive understanding of Life.

For when I say Flesh I say, above all, *apprehension*, hair standing on end, flesh naked with all the intellectual deepening of this spectacle of pure flesh, and all the consequences in the senses, that is, in feeling.

And whoever says feeling says intuition, that is, direct knowledge, communication turned inside out to its source to be clarified interiorly. There's a mind in the flesh but a mind quick as lightning. And yet the perturbation of the flesh partakes of the high substance of the mind.

And yet whoever says flesh also says sensibility. Sensibility, that is, assimilation. But an intimate, secret, profound assimilation, absolute in relation to my own suffering, and consequently a solitary and unique consciousness of this suffering.

*Translated by Daisy Aldan*

# INQUEST

YOU LIVE, YOU DIE. WHAT HAS FREE WILL GOT TO DO WITH IT ALL?
IT SEEMS YOU KILL YOURSELF THE WAY YOU HAVE A DREAM.
THIS IS NO MORAL QUESTION WE ARE ASKING:

## IS SUICIDE A SOLUTION?

No, suicide is still an hypothesis. I claim the right to be skeptical about suicide, just as I am skeptical about all the rest of reality. For the moment, and pending further orders, *one must* be frightfully skeptical, not about existence itself, which anybody at all can grasp, but rather about the inward agitation and profound feelings in things, in acts, in reality. I believe in nothing I am not joined to by the tangible and meteoric umbilical cord of my own thoughts. Even so, too many of my meteors are out of action. And I am vexed by other men's sentient blueprints of existence, and I resolutely abominate all reality. Suicide is no more than the fabulous and distant conquest of clear-thinking men, but suicide itself as a state of being is absolutely incomprehensible to me. An invalid doing himself in would be utterly without representational value, but the state of soul of a man who planned his suicide well, down to the material circumstances, the exact minute of undoing, would be marvelous. I have no idea what things really are, no idea of any human state; nothing of this world turns for me, nothing turns in me. Being alive, I suffer horribly. I fail to reach any existing state. And most certainly I died long ago; my suicide has already taken place. That is, I have already *been suicided*. But what would you think of an *anterior state of suicide*, a suicide that would make us retrace our steps on the yonder side of existence rather than the side of death. For that would be the only suicide that might make sense to me. I feel no hunger for death; I simply hunger *not to be,* never to have dropped into this sink of imbecilities, abdications, renunciations, and obtuse contacts which make up the conscious self of Antonin Artaud and are even weaker than he is. The conscious self of this wandering invalid, who from time to time keeps trying to exhibit his shadow, which he himself spat on long ago; this self on

60

crutches, limping along; this virtual, impossible self which nevertheless is part of reality. None like him ever felt his weakness, yet his weakness is the most important weakness of all mankind. To be destroyed, not to exist.

*Translated by David Rattray*

# GENERAL SECURITY — THE LIQUIDATION OF OPIUM

I have the not-dissimulated intention of finishing with this question so we shall no longer be bugged by the so-called dangers of the drug.

My point of view is clearly anti-social.

There is only one reason to attack opium. It is the fear that its use may become general throughout society.

*Now this danger is false.*

We are born rotten in the body and in the soul, we are congenitally unadapted; by suppressing opium you won't suppress the need for crime, the cancers of the body and of the soul, the propensity for despair, inborn stupidity, hereditary smallpox, the friability of the instincts. You won't be able to stop souls from being predestined for poison, whatever kind it might be: poison of morphine, poison of reading, poison of isolation, poison of onanism, poison of repeated coitus, poison of the rooted weakness of the soul, poison of alcohol, poison of tobacco, poison of anti-sociability. There are souls that are incurable and lost to the rest of society. If you take away from them a means of madness, they will invent ten thousand more. They will create means more subtle, more furious, absolutely *desperate*. Nature herself is anti-social in her soul, and it is not only through an usurpation of powers that the organized social body can react against humanity's *natural* fallout.

Let the lost get lost. We have other, much better, things to do with our time than to attempt an impossible regeneration which, besides, is useless, *hateful and injurious*.

As long as we haven't been able to abolish a single cause of human desperation, we do not have the right to try to suppress the means by which man tries to clean himself of desperation.

For it would be necessary first to get to suppress this natural and hidden impulse, this *plausible* inclination of man which leads him to find a way, which gives him the *idea* that he might look for a means of getting out of his troubles.

And even more, the lost are lost by nature, and all the ideas of moral regeneration won't do anything about it. There is *an innate determinism*, there is an indisputable incurability about suicide, crime, idiocy, madness; there is an invincible cuckoldom of man, a fallout of character; there is a castration of the mind.

Loss of speech exists, the tabes dorsalis exists, and so do syphilitic meningitis, robbery, usurpation. Hell is already of this world and there are men who are unhappy runaways from hell, runaways destined to repeat their escape *eternally*. And enough of this!

Man is miserable, the soul is weak, there are men who shall always get lost. The means for the lost do not matter; *it is not society's business.*

We have shown well, haven't we, that society can do nothing about it, that it is wasting its time, and that it should no longer persist in being rooted in its own stupidity.

And, in short, *injurious.*

For those who dare face the truth, we know, don't we, the results of the suppression of alcohol in the United States.

A superproduction of madness: beer on a diet of ether; alcohol larded with cocaine, which is sold secretly; multiplied drunkenness, a sort of general drunkenness. *In short, the law of the forbidden fruit.*

The same for opium.

This interdiction which multiplies curiosity for the drug and benefits only the pimps of medicine, or journalism and literature. There are people who have built excremental and famous industries out of their pretended indignation against an inoffensive group of the damned of the drug (inoffensive because so small and always — exceptional), this minority of beings damned by the mind, by the soul, by disease.

Oh, how well the umbilical cord of morality is tied in them. Since their mothers they have never, have they, sinned. They are the apostles, the descendants of the ministers of the gospel; we can only ask ourselves where they draw their indignation from and, above all, how much they have felt by such goings-on and, in any case, what their indignation has done for them.

And, besides, this isn't the question.

In reality, this fury against toxics, and the stupid law that follows it:

1) *is without effect against the need for toxics* which, satisfied or not, is innate to the soul and would induce it to resolutely antisocial gestures, *even if the toxics did not exist*;

2) *exasperates the social need for toxics* and changes it into a secret vice;

3) *is harmful to the real disease,* because this is the real question, the vital knot, the danger-point:

*Unfortunately for illness,* medicine does exist.

All the laws, all the restrictions, all the campaigns against narcotics will only lead to taking from those in pain and human need, who have irreducible rights over the social state, the solvent of their ills, a food more marvelous to them than bread, and the means at last for their repenetration into life.

Better the plague than morphine, yells official medicine, better hell than life. Only idiots like J. P. Liausu (who besides is an ignorant abortion) pretend that it is necessary to let the *sick soak in their illness*.

And this is where all the vulgar pedantry of certain people shows its hand and gives itself free rein: *in the name of the general good!*

Kill yourself, you who are desperate and you who are tortured in body and soul, lose all hope. There is no more relief for you in this world. The world lives on your graves.

And you, lucid madmen, consumptives, cancer-ridden, chronic meningitics, you are the misunderstood. There is a point in you that no doctor will ever understand and it is this point which, for me, saves you and makes you majestic, pure and marvelous: you are outside life, you are above life, you have pains which the ordinary man does not know, you go beyond the normal level and this is why men are against you, you are poisoning their quietude, you are the dissolvers of their stability. You have irrepressible pains, the essence of which is that they are unadaptable to any known state, incomprehensible to words. You have repeated and unceasing pains, insoluble pains, pains beyond thought, pains which are neither in the body nor the soul, *but which belong to both.* And as for me, I participate in your ills, and I ask you: who dares measure the tranquilizer for you? In the name of what superior light, soul to soul, can they understand us, we who are at the very root of knowledge and of clarity. And this on account of our insistence, our persistence in suffering. We, whom pain makes journey into our souls in search of a calm place to cling to, in search of stability in evil, as the others search for it in good — we aren't mad, we're marvelous doctors, we know the necessary dose for the soul, for sensibility, for the marrow, for thought. We want to be left in peace, the sick must be left in peace, we ask nothing of men, we ask only for relief of our ills. We have well evaluated our life, we know how much restriction it contains confronted by others, and especially confronted by ourselves. We know to what willing flabbiness, to what renunciation of ourselves, to what paralysis of subtleties our malady forces us every day. We are not committing suicide right away. Let us be left in peace in the meanwhile.

*Translated by L. Dejardin*


# ADDRESS TO THE DALAI LAMA

We are your most faithful servants, O Grand Lama, give us, grace us with your illuminations in a language our contaminated European minds can understand, and if need be, transform our Mind, create for us a mind turned entirely toward those perfect summits where the Human Mind no longer suffers.

Make us a Mind without habits, a mind truly frozen in the Mind, or a Mind with purer habits, your habits, if they can help us toward freedom.

We are surrounded by bellowing popes, poetasters, critics, dogs, our Mind is gone to the dogs who think directly in terms of the earth, who think incorrigibly in the present.

Teach us, O Lama, the physical levitation of matter and how we may no longer be earthbound.

For you well know what transparent liberation of souls, what freedom of the Mind in the Mind we mean, O acceptable Pope, O true Pope in the Mind.

With the inward eye I contemplate you, O Pope on the inward summit. It is inwardly that I am like you: I, dust, idea, lip, levitation, dream, cry, renunciation of idea, suspended among all the forms and hoping for nothing but the wind.

*Translated by David Rattray*

# NO THEOGONY . . .

No theogony is more effervescent and efficient than that of the three Gods:

TEZCTLIPOCA — HUICHIBOLOCH — QUETZALCOATL.

I mean to say that in a country where underground fiery forces burn naked, where the air bursting with birds vibrates at a higher pitch than anywhere else, created by the very fact, and by the power of things, of Gods.

And these Gods in turn produce a science in which astrology has its place.

We have much to learn from the secrets of Mexican astrology, as read and interpreted on the spot through heiroglyphs not yet deciphered.

Much to learn from a kind of diffuse consciousness — which there belongs to everyone — in a period when all countries of the world, Russia first, seek to construct a collective dynamism.

My mission, if mission there is, would consist of revealing and fixing

this dynamism as in Heraclitus' philosophy:
EARTH, symbolized by Volcanos and Snakes;
WATER, symbolized by multiple Gods, the infinite faces of
Tlaloc, and feathers of birds roaming the storms;
AIR, symbolized by slings of birds — from the Thunderbird
to the Zuetzal bird — the most precious of all sky-birds;
FIRE, symbolized again by the Thunderbird and by the volutes
of volcanos;
these four ELEMENTS, perpetually animated, finally reveal a magic
naturalism AND CLEARLY.

It is a spasmodic civilization, the living and concrete realization of
a philosophy.

I do not believe that any other civilization in the world presents ex-
amples as clear and animated as these. It seems that the flayed organs
perpetually expose the soul.

The civilization of the VEDAS among others preserves within it-
self, and in a rather extra-organic manner, an idea similar to that of
heaven.

There is, then, a wealth of reality to be drawn from the example of
Mexican civilization. It is in that direction that we intend to work.

If the civilization of Mexico offers a perfect example of the magic
spirit of primitive civilizations, we shall extract from it all forms of
primitive and magic culture that such a civilization can furnish, from
totemism to magic spell, while passing through astrological hierarchies,
rituals of water, fire, corn and snakes, cure by music and by plants,
apparitions in forests, etc . . .

We shall explain why the Mexicans have such fear of shadows and
of night in the forests.

I shall not pursue these points any further. I believe I have said
enough to show the purpose of the mission I request, and I only ask
and hope that you will support it and help to make of it a success.

*Translated by Raymond Federman*

# IT IS THE ACT WHICH SHAPES THE THOUGHT . . .

## [A Fragment]

. . . It is the act which shapes the thought. As for matter and mind, the Mexicans know only the concrete. And the concrete never tires of functioning, of drawing something from nothing: this is the secret we want to go and ask of the descendants of high Mexican civilizations.

Upon some lost plateaus, we shall interrogate healers and sorcerers, and we shall hope to hear the painters, poets, architects, sculptors state that they possess the whole reality of the images they have created — a reality which drives them on. For the secret of high Mexican magic lies in the power of signs created by those who in Europe would still be called artists, and who in advanced civilizations have not lost contact with natural sources and are the sole performers and prophets of a speech in which, periodically, the world must come to quench its thirst. Mexico can still teach us the secret of a diction and a language, where all dictions and languages gather in one.

If the civilization now rising in Mexico does not succeed in gaining consciousness of this multitude of expressions agglomerated around a unique center — expressions which derive from speech, syntax, form, gestures, and screams — it will prove itself incapable of finding the link with its genuine tradition.

In order to apprehend language, all languages, and avoid a universal chaos of languages, there is a key which can unlock all means of expressions.

The Mayas knew a type of hieroglyph which speaks and can be understood on several levels of meanings. To free the Indians, today, of Spanish constraint, has no meaning, if only to free them materially, unless the return to a pre-Cortesian civilization also signifies a return to cultural sources from which the ancient Maya civilization came forth.

Old Mexicans did not separate culture from civilization, nor culture from a personal knowledge distributed in the whole human organism.

It is in their organs and senses that the Mexicans, like all pure races, had learned to bear their culture, which achieved a refinement of sensitivity in the last degree and highest level.

One must note that the lowest Maya barbarian, the most remote Indian peon carries this culture in him like an atavism; and with this culture, which provides him with an inner knowledge noticeable in the exacerbation of his whole nervous system, the illiterate Indian is, when confronted with an European, similar to a civilized man of the highest rank: and this is the truth, the importance of which, we feel, must be affirmed. . . .

The conclusion to all of this can only be found on the spot, and it is important to recognize that which in modern rituals can subsist from ancient magic and ancient divination.

Are there still forests which speak? Where can sorcerers with burning fibres of Peyote and Marijuana still encounter that terrible old man who discloses the secrets of divination?

If Mexicans give such deep importance to the sky; if flying birds symbolize their violent desire for freedom and space, and their scorn of common reality, and, in a word, of life; if a prophecy promises them in a near future the awakening of the Thunderbird in the uproar of volcanos, the question remains as to which point this marv. . .

*Translated by Raymond Federman*

# CONCERNING A JOURNEY TO
# THE LAND OF THE TARAHUMARAS

## The Mountain of Signs

The land of the Tarahumara is full of signs, shapes, and natural effigies which do not seem to be mere products of accident, as if the gods, whose presence here is everywhere felt, had wished to signify their powers through these strange signatures in which the human form is hunted down from every side.

Indeed, there is no lack of places on earth where Nature, impelled by a kind of intelligent caprice, has carved human shapes. But here it is a different matter: for here it is on the entire *geographic area of a race* that Nature *has intentionally spoken.*

And the strange fact is that those who pass this way, as if stricken with an unconscious paralysis, seal their senses so as to know nothing of this. That Nature, by a strange caprice, should quite suddenly reveal a man's body being tortured on a rockface, one might at first suppose to be a mere caprice, a caprice signifying nothing. But when, day in and day out on horseback, this intelligent spell is cast repeatedly, and *Nature stubbornly manifests the same idea;* when the same pathetic shapes recur; when the heads of well-known gods appear on the rockfaces and a theme of death emerges of which man bears the burden — and in response to the drawn and quartered form of the human, there are, *becoming less obscure* and more freed from a petrifying substance, those forms of the gods who have forever tormented him, — when a whole country develops on stone a philosophy parallel to that of men; when one realizes that the original men used a sign language and that one rediscovers this language enormously magnified on the rocks, then indeed, one can no longer suppose this to be a caprice, a mere caprice signifying nothing.

If the major part of the Tarahumara race is indigenous, and if, as they claim, they fell out of the sky in the Sierra, one could say that they fell into a Nature already prepared. And this Nature wanted to think as man thinks. And as she *evolved* from men, likewise she also *evolved* from rocks.

I saw this naked man they were torturing, nailed to a rock, with certain forms at work over him even as the sun was evaporating them; but I don't know by what miracle of optics the man beneath them remained complete, though exposed to the same light.

Whether it was the mountain or myself which was haunted, I cannot say, but I saw similar optical miracles during this periplus across the mountain, and they confronted me at least once every day.

Maybe I was born with a body as tortured and counterfeited as that of the immense mountain; but it was a body whose obsessions might be useful: and it occurred to me in the mountain that it might be just useful to have an *obsession for counting*. There wasn't a shadow but I had it counted, when I sensed it turning, hovering around something or other; and it frequently happened that in adding up these shadows I made my way back to some strange hearths.

I saw in the mountain a naked man leaning out of a huge window. His head was nothing but an enormous hole, a sort of circular cavity, where successively and according to the hour, the sun or moon appeared. He had his right arm outstretched like a bar, and the left was also like a bar but drowned in shadows and folded inward.

His ribs could be counted, there were seven on either side. In place of his navel, there gleamed a brilliant triangle, made of what? I could not really tell. It was as if Nature had chosen this mountainside to lay bare her imprisoned flints.

Now, though his head was empty, the indentations of the rock on every side imposed on him a definite expression, the nuances of which changed with the changes of hour and light.

This forward stretching right arm, edged with a ray of light, did not indeed point in any commonplace direction . . . And I questioned what it portended!

It was not quite noon when I encountered this vision; I was on horseback and rapidly advancing. However, I was instantly aware that I was not dealing with graven images, but with a predetermined play of light which had *superimposed itself* upon the stone relief.

This likeness was known to the Indians; to me, it appeared by its composition, its structure, to be governed by the same principle by which this fragmented mountain was governed. In the line that arm made, I saw a rock-girt village.

And I saw that the stones all had the shape of a woman's bosom with two breasts perfectly delineated.

Eight times I saw the repetition of a single rock, which cast two shadows on the ground; I twice saw the same animal head holding its own likeness in its jaws and devouring it; I saw, dominating the village, a sort of huge phallic tooth with three stones at its summit and four holes on its outer face; and I saw, according to their principle, all these forms pass little by little into reality.

I seemed to read everywhere a tale of childbirth amid war, a tale of genesis and chaos, with all these bodies of gods which were carved like men, and these truncated human statues. Not one shape that was intact, not one body that did not appear as if it came out of a recent massacre, not one group where I could avoid reading the struggle that divided it.

I found drowned men, half-nibbled away by the stones, and on the rocks higher up, other men engaged in driving them off. Elsewhere, a statue of Death loomed huge, holding in its hand a little child.

There is in the Kabbala a music of Numbers, and this music which reduces material chaos to its prime elements explains by a kind of grandiose mathematics how Nature orders and directs the birth of forms she brings forth out of chaos. And all I beheld seemed to be governed by a Number. The statues, the shapes, the shadows all yielded a number, — such as 3, 4, 7, or 8, — which kept recurring. The truncated female torsos were 8 in number; the phallic tooth had, as I have said, three stones and four holes; the evaporated forms were 12 in number, et cetera. I repeat, these forms may be assumed natural, granted, but their repetition is far from natural. And what is even less natural is that these forms of their land are repeated by the Tarahumara in their rituals and dance. And these dances result from no mere accident, but they are governed by the same secret mathematics, the same concern for a subtle play of Numbers which governs the entire Sierra.

Now this inhabited Sierra, which breathes a metaphysical system into its rocks, has been strewn by the Tarahumara with signs, signs which are perfectly conscious, intelligent, and concerted.

At every crossroads one sees trees *deliberately* burnt into the shape of crosses, or of beings, and often these beings are doubles, and confront each other, as if to express the essential *duality* of things; and I saw this duality reduced to its prime elements in a sign . . . enclosed in a ring, which struck me as having been branded on a tall pine tree with a red-hot iron; other trees bore spears, trefoils, acanthus leaves surrounded with crosses; here and there, in sunken places, corridors choked with rocks, rows of Egyptian ankhs deployed in files; and the doors of Tarahumara houses displayed the Maya world-symbol: two facing triangles whose points are joined by a bar; and this bar is the Tree of Life passing through the center of Reality.

Thus, as I was making my way across the mountain, these spears, these crosses, these trefoils, these leafy hearts, these composite crosses, these triangles, these beings which confront and oppose each other to signify their eternal war, their division, their duality, awakened in me strange memories. I recall suddenly that there were in History certain Sects which had incrusted the rockfaces with identical signs, and the members of these Sects wore these signs carved in jade, hammered in iron, or chased. And it occurs to me that this symbolism hides a Science. And it seems strange to me that the primitive Tarahumara people, whose rituals and thought are older than the Flood, could have already possessed this Science long before the first Legend of the Graal appeared, long before the Rosecrucian Sect was founded.

### The Peyote Dance

The physical compression was still there. This cataclysm that was my body . . . After waiting twenty-eight days, I had still not come to myself — I should instead say: *come out* into myself. Into myself, within this dilapidated shambles, this ramshackle piece of deteriorated geology.

Inert, as some earth with its rocks can be inert — and all these crevices which run in the huddled sedimentary strata. Friable is the word for it — I was; and not just in some places, but through and through. Ever since first coming in contact with this terrible mountain, which

72

I am sure had erected barriers against me to bar my entry. And since my experience there, the supernatural no longer seems so extraordinary to me that I may not affirm that I was, in the literal sense of the word, *bewitched*.

Taking a step was for me no longer a matter of taking a step, but a feeling *which way* to point my head. Is this understood? Limbs which obey, one by one, and are advanced, one by one; the aboveground and vertical posture to be maintained. For the head, overflowing with waves and no longer in control of its own rotations, feels the rotations of the earth, and this drives it to distraction and bars it from staying upright.

Twenty-eight days of this ponderous compression, of this mess of badly assembled organs that was me, and of which I seemed a mere spectator, as if I gazed upon an immense glacial landscape at the verge of breaking up.

So the pressure was there and it was so terrible that in order to go from the Indian's house to a tree standing scarcely a few yards off, I needed something more than courage, I had to muster the truly *desperate* reserves of my will power. For having come so far, to find myself at last on the threshold of an encounter and of this place I had hoped so many revelations from, and then to feel so forlorn, so empty, so un-crowned. Had I ever known joy, had there ever been in this world one single feeling not of anguish or of inexpiable despair; had I ever known a state other than this grief cracking up and pursuing me through the nights? Was there anything for me that was not at the door of agony and should I contact at least one body, one single human body safe from my perpetual crucifixion?

Indeed, I needed willpower to believe something would happen. And all of this, for what? For a dance, for a ritual of some lost Indians who didn't even know who they were anymore, nor where they came from, and who, when I questioned them, answered me with stories whose mystery and coherence they had garbled.

After labors, I repeat, so cruel that I can no longer believe that I was not actually bewitched, that these barriers of collapse and cataclysm I had felt rising in me were not the result of an intelligent and concerted premeditation, I reached one of the last places on earth where the Peyote medicine dance still exists, the place, in any case, where it was invented. And yet what was it, what false intimation, what illusory and spurious intuition had led me to expect from it some sort of liberation for my body, and also, above all, a strength, an illumination throughout the width of my internal landscape, which at this very minute I felt to be quite outside all possible dimensions?

Twenty-eight days since this inexplicable torture had begun. And twelve days since I had been in this isolated corner of earth, in this walled-in compartment of the immense mountain, awaiting the pleasure of my sorcerers.

Why was it that every time, like now, when I felt I was reaching a crucial phase of my existence, I never could get there in one piece with my whole being? Why this terrible feeling of loss, of something lacking to be made up for, of a happening that miscarried somehow? Indeed, I would see the sorcerers perform their ritual; but what good would this ritual do me? I would see them. I would be compensated for this long patience that nothing so far had been able to dishearten. Nothing: neither the terrible road, nor the journey with this intelligent but unattuned body which had to be dragged, which should be killed almost in order to prevent it from rising up against me; neither nature with her storms which enmesh us in their sudden nets of lightning; nor this long spasm-crossed night, during which I saw an Indian boy scratch himself (while dreaming with a sort of hateful frenzy) at exactly the places where those spasms crossed my body — and he said, who only a day earlier had scarcely known me: " Ah, have everything bad that can happen happen to him! "

Peyote, I knew, was none of White men's business. So I must at all costs be prevented from getting a cure from this ritual devised to act on the very nature of the spirits. And a White, to these Red men, is one the spirits have forsaken. If I got any good out of the ritual, it was so much the less for them, with their intelligent spirit-lining.

So much the less for the spirits. So many more spirits they could no longer take advantage of.

And then, there is the question of *Tesguino,* this corn liquor it takes eight days to macerate in jars — and there are neither jars nor willing hands enough to grind the corn.

The liquor drunk, the Peyote sorcerers are of no further use, and a whole new preparation has to be gone through. Now, a man of these tribes had died when I arrived at the village, and it was required that the ritual, the priests, the liquor, the crosses, the mirrors, the graters, the jars and all the extraordinary apparatus of the Peyote dance be directed for the benefit of the man who had died. For, once he was dead, his double could not wait for those evil spirits to be got rid of.

And after twenty-eight days of waiting, I still had to endure a whole long week more of the most incredible farce. The mountain went wild with the comings and goings of messengers supposedly in touch with the sorcerers. But no sooner would the messengers leave, than the sorcerers would arrive on the scene and get indignant that nothing was happening. And I realized they were putting me on.

They brought me priests who were dream-healers and spoke after dreaming.

' Those of the *Ciguri* (Peyote dance) no good,' they said. ' They no *use*. You take these.' And they thrust on me these old men that would suddenly get the bends and jiggle their amulets in a queer way under their robes. And I saw they were palming off jugglers — not sorcerers — on me. And I learned these fake priests were intimate friends of the dead man.

One day the excitement cooled; there were no screams, no arguments, no more renewed promises on my behalf. As if all that had been just part of the ritual, and now the preliminaries had lasted long enough.

Indeed, I had not penetrated the heart of the mountain of these Tarahumara Indians in search of memories of painting. I had suffered long enough, I thought, to deserve a little reality.

Nevertheless, as night drew on, a vision possessed my eyes.

I had before me the Nativity of Hieronymus Bosch, arranged in order and turned so the old uneven clapboard roof was sloping down in front of the stable, with the flames of the Child-King gleaming on the left among the animals, with the scattered farms, the shepherds;

and, in the foreground, other animals bleating; and, on the right, the dancer-kings. The kings, with their mirror-crowns on their heads and their rectangular purple robes on their backs — to my right in the picture — like the Magi of Hieronymus Bosch. And all of a sudden, as I was turning around, doubting to the last of ever really seeing my sorcerers arrive, I saw them coming down the mountain, leaning on their huge staffs, and their wives with huge baskets, and a retinue armed with crosses loosely bundled like fasces or trees, their mirrors gleaming like patches of sky amid this vast array of crosses, pikes, spades and lopped treetrunks. And this whole crowd was bending under the weight of such an extraordinary array, and the sorcerers' wives like their husbands were a head shorter than the great staffs they leaned on.

Bonfires rose on all sides in the sky. Below, the dancing had already begun; and confronted with this beauty at last achieved, this beauty of imaginations radiant as voices in an illuminated cave beneath the earth, I felt that my efforts had not been in vain.

Higher up, on the sides of the immense mountain which were falling in terraces toward the village, a ring of earth had been traced. Already the women kneeling before their *metates* (stone vats) were grinding the Peyote with a sort of scrupulous brutality. The officiants started to tread down the ring. They treaded it out carefully and in all directions; and they kindled in the center of this ring a pyre which the wind from aloft sucked swirling upwards.

During that day, two kid goats had been slaughtered. And now I saw on a lopped treetrunk, it too hewn into a cruciform, the animals' lungs and hearts quivering in the night wind.

Another lopped treetrunk stood next to the first, and the bonfire in the circle's midst produced in it innumerable glints and glimmers, something like a conflagration seen through very thick, dense layers of broken glass. I drew nearer, to determine the nature of this focal point, and I perceived an incredible tangle of little bells, some silver, some horn, attached to leather jesses, and awaiting the moment when they too would act their role in the exercises.

Facing the quarter of the sunrise, they raised ten crosses of irregular size, but all lined up in symmetrical order: and to each cross they attached a mirror.

Twenty-eight days of this horrible waiting after the dangerous constraint now culminated in a ring inhabited with Beings, here represented by ten crosses.

Ten, to the Number of Ten, like the Invisible Lords of the Peyote in the Sierra.

And among these ten: the Male Principle of Nature, which the Indians named *Saint Ignatius,* and its female, *Saint Nicolas!*

Around this ring, a zone morally deserted, in which no Indian would venture: they say that birds that stray into this ring fall, and pregnant women feel their embryos decompose.

A history of the world is danced here in the round, squeezed between two suns, the setting and the rising. And so it is, in the setting sun, the sorcerers enter the ring, and the dancer with six hundred little bells (300 of horn, 300 of silver) shrieks his coyote call in the forest.

The dancer goes in and out, yet never quits the ring. He deliberately advances into Evil. He plunges into it headlong and with a sort of hideous courage, in a rhythm which transcends the Dance but seems graphic of Disease. And we imagine we see him emerging and vanishing by turns, with a movement suggestive of I know not what obscure tantalizations. He goes in and out: 'To go forth by day, in the first chapter,' says the Egyptian Book of the Dead, of the Human Double. For this advance into disease is a journey, a *descent* in order to GO OUT AGAIN BY DAY. He spins round and round like the wings of the Swastika, forever right to left, top foremost.

He leaps with his army of little bells, such a swarm of frantic bees, stuck fast to one another, rustling blind in a crackling and tempestuous disorder.

*Ten* crosses in the ring and *ten* mirrors. *One* beam with three sorcerers on it. *Four* officiants (*two* Males and *two* Females). The epileptic dancer, and ME for whom this ritual was made.

At each sorcerer's feet, *one* hole, at the bottom of which the Male and Female of Nature, represented by the hermaphroditic roots of the Peyote (the Peyote, as we well know, bears the form of a man and

77

woman's genital mingled), are sleeping in Matter, that is, in the Concrete.

And the hole, with a wooden or earthen bowl turned upsidedown over it, represents fairly well the world-Sphere. On this bowl the sorcerers grate the merging or separating of the two principles, and they grate them in the Abstract, that is, in their prime elements or Principle. Meanwhile, underneath these, these two Principles are embodied and repose in Matter, that is, in the Concrete.

And the whole night through, these sorcerers restore lost rapports, with triangular gestures which strangely intersect the air's perspectives.

Between the *two* suns, *twelve* periods in *twelve* phases. And the procession round and round of all that swarms about the pyre, within the sacred limits of the ring: the dancer, the graters, the sorcerers.

Between the phases, the sorcerers were eager to get physical proof of the ritual, of the efficacy of the operation. Hieratic, ritual, sacerdotal, there they go, filing back and forth on the beam, cradling their grater like a babe. From what conceptions of a lost etiquette do they get the sense of these bows and courtsies, and of their marching round and round as they count their steps and cross themselves in front of the flames, saluting one another and going out?

So they get up and go through the bowings I have mentioned, some like men on crutches, others like decapitated robots. They jump out of the ring. But once out of it, scarcely a yard outside, these priests, moving between two suns, are suddenly turned back into human beings, that is, organisms of abjection that have to be washed, and this ritual is for the purpose of washing them. They act like sewermen, these priests, like some sort of toilers in darkness, created to piss and throw up. They do piss and fart and throw up with dreadful thunderings; you would think, then, to hear them, that they wanted to debase real thunder by adjusting it to *their need* for abjection.

Of the three sorcerers present, two, the two smaller and shorter, had three years previously won the right to handle the grater (for the right to handle the grater must be won, and besides it is upon this privilege that the whole nobility of the caste of Peyote Sorcerers reposes among the Indians of the Tarahumara); and the third priest had won the right

78

ten years before. And it was the oldest in the rite who, I must say, pissed best and farted most ardently and loudest.

And this same one, with a conceit born of this kind of uncouth purgation, started spitting a few moments later. He spat after having drunk the Peyote like all the rest of us. For the twelve phases of the dance were done, and as dawn was about to break, we were handed the grated Peyote, which looked like some kind of slimy chowder; and in front of each of us a fresh hole was dug to receive the sputum and vomit of our mouths, which had been made holy by the Peyote's passing through.

' Spit! ' said the dancer to me. ' But spit as deep in the ground as you can, for not one bit of *Cigouri* must ever come up again.'

And it was the sorcerer grown old in harness who spat up the most copiously and in the thickest, heaviest gobs. And the other sorcerers with the dancer huddled around his hole to admire this.

Soon after spitting, I began to fall asleep. The dancer in front of me never stopped passing to and fro, whirling and screaming *superfluously*, because he had discerned that I took pleasure in his screaming.

' Get up, man, get up! ' he shrieked, with each of his more and more futile gyrations.

Awakened and staggering, I was led toward the crosses for the final cure, in which the sorcerers rattle the graters on the patient's very head.

Then I shared in the water ritual, in blows on the skull, in this sort of mutual healing passed back and forth, and ablutions beyond measure.

They pronounced strange words over me and sprinkled me with water; then they sprinkled one another nervously, for the mixture of corn liquor and Peyote was starting to make them crazy, too.

And it was with these last passes that the Peyote dance ended.

The Peyote dance is inside a grater, in its time-tempered wood, endowed with the occult salts of the earth. It is in the taut and involuted fibres of this wand that the healing virtues of the rite dwell, and it is so complex, so withdrawn, it must be hunted and tracked down

79

like some beast in the forest.

There is, it seems, a certain cranny in the high Mexican Sierra, where these graters abound. They sleep there, waiting for the Pre-destined Man to discover them and make them *go forth by day.*

Each Tarahumara sorcerer, when dying, abandons his grater with infinitely more pain than it takes him to abandon his body; and his children and intimates carry the grater out and bury it in that sacred corner of the forest.

When a Tarahumara Indian feels himself called to the vocation of the grater and the healing dance, he comes for three consecutive Easters to spend a week in the woods.

It is there, they say, that the Invisible Lord of the Peyote speaks to him with his nine Assessors, and hands down the secret to him. And he goes forth again with the grater duly macerated.

Carved from a wood of the warm zones, gray as iron ore, this wand bears notches from end to end, and signs on either end: four triangles, with one dot for the Male Principle and two dots for the deified Female of Nature.

As many notches as the sorcerer had years when he acquired the right to grate and became also free to practice the exorcisms by which the Elements are drawn and quartered.

And this is just the side of the mysterious tradition which I never succeeded in penetrating. For the Peyote sorcerers seem to have really acquired something at the end of their three years of retreat in the woods.

Here we have a mystery the Tarahumara sorcerers have so far jea-lously guarded. Of what else they have acquired, of what they have so to speak *recovered,* no Tarahumara Indian outside the aristocracy seems to have the slightest idea. And, as for the sorcerers themselves, they remain resolutely silent on this point.

What is the singular word, that lost utterance, the Lord of the Peyote passes down to them? And why do they need three years to handle the grater properly, this grater on which, it must be admitted, the Tarahumara sorcerers perform some rather curious *auscultations?*

What is it, then, they have torn from the forest and the forest *yields to them so slowly?*

What, finally, has been handed down to them that is not of the outward array of the ritual, and which neither the gimlet screams of the dancer, nor his double moving back and forth like some kind of epileptic pendulum, nor the ring, nor the pyre at the center of the ring, nor the crosses with their mirrors dangling in which the deformed heads of the sorcerers are now distended and now vanished amid the flaming pyre, nor the night wind speaking and breathing on the mirrors, nor the litany of the sorcerers cradling their graters, that astoundingly vulnerable and revulsed litany — what is it that none of these can succeed in explaining.

They had lain me down on the ground itself, at the foot of the enormous beam on which the three sorcerers sat, in the breaks between dances.

Lain me down low, so the ritual would descend upon me, so that fire, litany, screams, dance and the night itself like a living human vault might wheel as a living being over me. So there was this rolling vault, this material intricacy of screams, tones, footsteps, litany. But above all, transcending all, this impression, which recurred, that behind all that, and more than all of it, and beyond it, still something else was hidden: namely, *the principle.*

I did not renounce all at once these dangerous disassociations it seems Peyote provokes, and which I had for years sought by other means; I did not mount on horseback with a body torn from itself and which the constraint I had imposed on myself had deprived of its essential reflexes; I had not been this man of stone it took two men to make into a man on horseback, and whom they hoisted on and off my horse like a broken robot — and once on horseback they put my hands on the reins, and in addition to that they had to close my fingers on the reins, for it was only too obvious that I had lost control; I had not conquered by force of spirit this invincible organic hostility, where it was *me* that did not want to continue, in order to bring back from it a collection of motheaten imagery, from which this Age, thus far faithful to a whole system, would at the very most get a few new ideas for posters and models for its fashion designers. From now on it

81

was necessary that whatever lay buried behind this ponderous tritura-
tion, which makes the dawn one with the dead of night, be dragged
out in the open and put to *use*, that it serve precisely for *my cruci-
fixion.*

To this, I knew my physical destiny was irremediably attached. I
was ready for every burning and I awaited the first fruits of burning,
in view of a soon-to-be generalized combustion.

Rodez, 7 September 1945

My dear Henri Parisot,

I wrote you at least three weeks ago a couple of letters instructing
you to publish the *Journey to the Land of the Tarahumaras,* but ap-
pending to it a letter replacing the *Supplement to the Journey,* in
which I was fool enough to say I had accepted conversion to Jesus
Christ, while in very fact Christ is that which I have always most of all
abominated, and this conversion was merely the result of a frightful
spell which had made me forget my very nature and had made me
swallow, at Rodez, under the guise of Communion, a frightful number
of wafers destined to preserve me for as long as possible, and if pos-
sible for all eternity, in a being that is not my own. This being con-
sists of ascending into the sky as a spirit instead of descending deeper
and deeper as a body into hell, that is into sexuality, soul of all that
lives. While that which is Christ carries the being away into the empy-
rean of clouds and gasses where since the beginning of time it has been
dissolving.

The ascension of the so-called Jesus Christ two thousand years ago
was nothing more than the ascension, in an infinite vertical line, in
which he one day ceased to be, and in which all that was left of him
devolved on the sex of all mankind as the basis of all lust. Like Jesus
Christ there is supposed also to be one who never would descend to
earth, because man was too small for him; and so he stayed in the
abysses of infinities, like some so-called immanence of God who in-
defatigably and like some Buddha in his self-contemplation awaits the
day that BEING will be sufficiently perfect for Him to descend into
it and slip inside it, which is the infamous scheming of a slothful and

82

cowardly rotter who would never have wanted to suffer the Being, the Being in its wholeness, but to make it suffer by proxy for another, in order subsequently to exorcise this wretched other, and relegate it to hell, when this mad visionary of anguish would have made out of the being of HIS suffering a paradise all prepared for this ghoul of sloth and villainy called God and Jesus Christ. I am one of these sufferers God has the nerve to lower himself to when I die, but I have three daughters who are three more of them, and I wish you to be also another one of them, in your soul, dear Parisot, because next to God and Christ there are angels with the same pretension he's got, who have forever claimed to share the consciousness of every being ever born, while they think themselves to be pure innateness. I want you to understand that it was not Jesus Christ I went looking for among the Tarahumara, but myself, me, Antonin Artaud, born September 4, 1896 at Marseille, 4 rue du Jardin des Plantes, out of a uterus I had nothing to do with and which I have never had a thing to do with even previously, for this is no way to be born, to be copulated and masturbated for nine months by the membrane, the yawning membrane which toothlessly devours, as the UPANISHADS say, and I know that I was born otherwise, born of my own works and not of a mother, but the MOTHER tried to get me and you have seen how that turned out in my life. I was born only in my own labor-pangs and if only you could do the same for yourself, dear Henri Parisot. As for these pangs, we must conclude they tasted good to the uterus, 49 years ago, for it tried to have them for itself, and has nourished itself on them in the guise of motherhood. And Jesus Christ is this thing born of a mother who also tried to get me for himself, and that long before the beginnings of time and the universe, and I went to the heights of Mexico only to rid myself of Jesus Christ, just as I plan on going some day to Tibet in order to flush god and his Holy Ghost out of me. Will you follow me there?

Publish this letter instead of the *Supplement,* and return the *Supplement,* if you please, to me. All best,

Antonin Artaud
*Translated by David Rattray*

83

# THE NEW REVELATIONS OF BEING

The fire in the water,
> the air in the earth,

the water in the air,
> and the earth in the sea.

They are not yet insane enough, they are not enough at each other's throats, and the more furious, the more enraged, the nearer and dearer they are.

Here where the Mother eats her sons,
Power eats Power:
Short of war, no stability.

> A mortal
> folly comes
> over the world
> for Man this
> night has been
> re-installed in
> the Absolute

> 8-8-37 = 8

> *to Madame Manuel Cano de Castro*


Translator's Note: This page and the two diagrams did not appear in the original edition but were added to Mme. Cano de Castro's copy by Artaud himself and later published by Manuel Cano de Castro as a key to *The New Revelations* in *K* (No. 1, 1947). It was Manuel Cano de Castro who taught Artaud the use of the Tarot, and the horoscopes for this book were cast in his presence. The interpretations are not 'classical' but personal.

*I say what I have seen and believe; and whoever says I have not seen what I have seen, I will now tear off his head.*

*For I am an unpardonable Brute, and so I shall be until Time is no longer Time.*

*Neither Heaven nor Earth, if they exist, can do anything against this brutality they have imposed upon me, perhaps that I might serve them . . . Who knows?*

*In any case, that I might be torn away from them.*

*I perceive, with certitude, that which is. That which is not shall be made by me, if necessary.*

*For a long time now I have felt the Void, but have refused to throw myself into the Void.*

*I have been as cowardly as all that I see.*

*When I believed I was refusing the world, I know now I was refusing the Void.*

*For I know that this world does not exist, and I know how and why it does not exist.*

*My sufferings until now consisted in refusing the Void.*

*The Void that was already in me.*

*I know there has been a wish to enlighten me by the Void and I have refused to let myself be enlightened.*

*If I was made into a pyre, it was intended to cure me of being in this world.*

*And the world took from me all I had.*

*I struggled in my attempt to exist, in my attempt to consent to the forms (all the forms) with which the delirious illusion of being in the world has clothed reality.*

*I no longer wish to be a Believer in Illusions.*

*Dead to the world; dead to that which is for everyone else the world, fallen at last, fallen, uplifted in this void that I once refused, I have a body that submits to the world, and disgorges reality.*

*I've had enough of this lunar movement that makes me name what I refuse and refuse what I have named.*

*I must put an end to it. I must at last make a clean break with this world which a Being in me, this Being I can no longer name because if he returns I shall fall into the Void, this Being has always refused.*

*It's done. I really fell into the Void after all — that makes this world — had achieved its purpose of making me despair.*

*For this knowledge of no longer being in this world comes only with seeing that the world has indeed left you.*

*Dead, the others have not been separated: they still hover around their corpses.*

*And I know how and why the dead have been hovering around their corpses for exactly the same thirty-three Centuries that my Double has been incessantly turning.*

*So, no longer existing, I see that which is.*

*I really identified myself with this Being, this Being that has ceased to exist.*

*And this Being revealed to me all things.*

*I knew it, but could not say it, and if I can start to say it now, it is because I have left reality behind.*

*This is a real Madman talking to you, one who never knew the happiness of being in the world until now that he has left it and become absolutely separated from it.*

*Dead, the others have not been separated. They still hover around their corpses.*

*I am not dead, but I am separated.*

I shall therefore speak what I have seen and what is.

And to say it, since the Astrologers no longer know how to read, I shall base myself on the Tarots.

# DIAGRAM OF HOROSCOPE OF SATURDAY
## JUNE 19, 1937 — *on the Initiate*

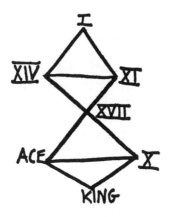

XIV  Temperance: self-mastery
I  Juggler, standing: properly directed will
XI  Strength: spiritual energy
XVII  Star of the Magi: regeneration
X  of Batons: harmony
King of Cups: domination
Ace of Cups: will at the service of the senses

HOROSCOPE OF SATURDAY, JUNE 19, 1937

HEAVEN

TERNARY

The Tarots have spoken in Heaven:
'THE ABSOLUTE MALE OF NATURE HAS BEGUN TO
MOVE IN THE HEAVENS. HE IS REVIVED FOR THE JUS-
TICE OF THE MALE. AND IT IS THE JUSTICE OF HEAVEN

THAT HAS REVIVED THE MALE THIS DAY.'
What does this mean?

It means that Man is to recover his stature. And that he will recover it against Men. It also means that a Man is to re-impose the Supernatural. Since the Supernatural is man's *raison d'être*. And man has betrayed the Supernatural.

It also means that, in a world given over to the sexuality of the woman, the spirit of man will recover its rights. It means finally that all that makes man has left us because we have betrayed man. And the Man in us has freed himself from the man. He has ascended to judge us for being men. And this is why we can no longer create. And we have no more than to look at ourselves to believe this.

## QUATERNARY

HEAVEN HAS INVOKED THE FORGOTTEN FEMININITY OF WOMAN. IT HAS USED A POWER THAT WOMAN HAD NEGLECTED.

IT HAS FORCED NATURE TO DREAM OF OPERATIONS THAT WOMAN CAN NO LONGER DREAM OF.

IT HAS FORCED NATURE TO BECOME WOMAN'S *proxy* IN ORDER TO ACHIEVE AN OPERATION PREPARED BY THE MALE.

What does this mean?
It means that nature is about to revolt.
Earth. Water. Fire. Heaven.
The transmutation will be performed by the four Elements gathered together.

## EARTH

The reclassification of all values will be fundamental, absolute, terrible.
But how will this terrible reclassification of values be performed?

By the four Elements, with Fire in the center, of course! But where, when, how, by what means, through what?

### TERNARY

'BY WOMAN. THROUGH WOMAN. BY WOMAN INDI-RECTLY ENLIGHTENED AND ACHIEVING HER OWN DUPLICITY. FOR IT WAS BY WOMAN THAT THE DIVIDER KING WAS SEPARATED WITHIN HIMSELF AND FOUND IN HIMSELF THE MEANS BY WHICH TO SEPARATE ALL THAT SHOULD BE SEPARATED.'

What does this mean?

This means:

### QUATERNARY

A natural force altered by woman will free itself against and by woman. This force is a death-force.

IT HAS THE DARK RAPACIOUSNESS OF THE GENITAL. IT IS PROVOKED BY WOMAN BUT MAN DIRECTS IT. THE MUTILATED FEMININITY OF MAN, THE ENCHAINED TENDERNESS OF MEN THAT WOMAN HAD STAMPED ON HAVE REVIVED A VIRGIN ON THAT DAY. BUT IT WAS A VIRGIN WITHOUT BODY, WITHOUT SEX, ONE WHICH ONLY THE MIND CAN PROFIT BY.

What does this mean?

It means that sexuality will be put in its place. In the place it should never have got out of. That the sexes will be for a time separated. That human love will be rendered impossible. And that this work is already begun.

It means that an Initiation will begin in the darkness.

It means that at the bottom of the present Destiny there was a treason on the part of woman. Not woman against some individual man, but woman against all men.

*And it means that Woman will return to Man.*

What does this mean?

It means that the world will be leveled by the Right. And that t.
Left will fall once more under the Supremacy of the Right. Not *here,*
or *elsewhere,* but EVERYWHERE.

Because a World-Cycle has closed that was under the supremacy
of Woman: the Left, the Republic, and Democracy.

It means that in the month of Cancer Death will reap all that is of
Cancer: the Left, the Republic and Democracy.

Because Cancer makes 69 and the Left does 69.

What else does this mean?

It means that a *superior Initiation* will be the fruit of this Death
and that all that has to do with sexuality will be burnt in this superior
Initiation, its fire transformed by Initiation.

In order to re-establish everywhere the absolute Supremacy of Man.

*And it means that man in Spirit above woman will once more direct
Life.*

It means that the Masses will everywhere fall once more under the
yoke, and that it is right that they should be under the yoke.

Because the Masses are Women by nature, and it is Man who go-
verns Woman, and not the contrary.

And until now poets have called this dominating Male: the Spirit.

So, what does this insolent prediction, the language of which no one
but visionaries and madmen will understand, mean?

It means that we are threatened with slavery, because Nature is
about to fall down around us.


That which makes us men and which has separated woman from
man is in the process of withdrawing from men,

of observing us and judging us.

All that permits us to exist and that sees how badly we have sub-
sisted and how badly we have kept the virile principle in us

leaves us, but in order to come down around us.

And the Virgin that it will concoct is the Natural Revolt of things
we have turned to ill use.

And the Revolution that we did not know how to make will be made by the Universe against us.

For Revolution, too, remembers that she is a woman,

And before restoring the Kings everywhere, Kings that will then be the slaves of all and will thereby know all the better how to keep the world enslaved.

This Revolution will teach us again, by her impossible possession, which will make every one of us possessed and insane,

HOW LIFE IS WITHDRAWING FROM US.

## HELL

By what path, by what means, by Whom, will this superior transmutation be performed?

### TERNARY

BY A MADMAN WHO IS ALSO A WISEMAN AND WHO HIMSELF SEES HE IS A WISEMAN AND A MADMAN.

What does this mean?

It means that he is balanced between Life and Solitude.

And that he has appeared to some as a Solitary Madman and Sage, and to others as an Extravagant Lout.

### QUATERNARY

BY HIM THE SEXES HAVE BEEN SEPARATED WITH THE FLAME, FOR HE KNEW BY NATURE THE FLAME OF LOVE WON AND LOST.

AND IN ORDER TO MAKE THEM ACCEPT THIS SEPARATION BY THE FLAME, HE FIRST PLAYED WITH HIS OWN FLAME.

AT FIRST HE PRETENDED TO BE AN EXTRAVAGANT LOUT.

AND THE DESTINY OF MAN AND THE UNIVERSE IS SUSPENDED BY THIS MOUNTEBANK OF A LOUT.

In how much time will this revolting transmutation, which can no longer be a Revolution, be performed?

In 5 months.

From what date?

The 3rd of June, 1937.

Why?

BECAUSE, ON THE THIRD OF JUNE, 1937, THE FIVE SER-PENTS APPEARED, WHO WERE ALREADY IN THE SWORD WHOSE STRENGTH OF DECISION IS REPRESENTED BY A STAFF!

What does this mean?

It means that I who am speaking have a Sword and a Staff.

A staff with 13 knots, and this staff bears on the ninth knot the magic sign of the thunderbolt; and 9 is the number of destruction by fire and

I FORESEE A DESTRUCTION

B Y  F I R E .

That is, an infernal destruction. And 9 is the number of infernal destruction, since hell represents fire.

I see this staff in the midst of the Fire, and this staff is provoking the destruction by Fire.

*And this destruction will be radical.*

I obtained the Sword from an African Negro, and the Staff from God.

This Staff, I have been told, was already mine in other centuries.

MY SWORD HAS THREE HOOKS AND SEVEN KNOTS.

So, out of the 5 Serpents that were revealed to me by absolutely ordinary means, 3 are in the shape of fangs, where I saw the hooks of the Sword. Another tapering where I saw the Sword. The last is shaped like a knot.

The first, who advances ahead of the others, rises like a wave and he is shaped like a fang. The two others, that seem to turn like a bundle of blazing rods, end in fangs, too.

The lower one has a point, as if the earth were heaving.

The top one advances through the air like a comet that will fall.

What does this mean?

It means that on June 3rd the powers of Heaven were set in motion.

It means that, on the 3rd of June last, an occult power of destruction began to gather, and on the 3rd of November it is to break forth.

Why?

Because 5 is the number of Man, not of men, but of the Abstract Man, and I have concluded that the destruction would be accomplished by man and *within* man and that it would take five months to get there.

For if I add the 3 of June 3rd to the number of the 6th month of the year, I obtain 9, the Infernal Destruction which began on that day.

If I add 5, number of the Abstract Man, to 6 of the 6th month of the year, I obtain 11, which brings me back to November, and November is under the sign of the number 9 according to the old calendar.

But November is the eleventh month of the year. And if, by Kabbalistically reducing the Numbers, I separate the two ones of 11 and undertake to add them, I obtain 2, which according to the Kabbala is the number of Separation-Destruction.

Moreover, the ciphers in 1937, added according to the same system of Kabbalistic reduction, give 2, likewise.

And the 5, of the Serpents and of the Abstract Man, added to the 6th month of the year, give another 11, bringing us back to November, and 11 of November reduces to 2.

Thus on all sides the Destruction everywhere sought has been unconsciously desired by everyone and I claim that it is secretly *willed* by everyone as the only means of saving us from a world where life can no longer function.

And this Destruction has begun everywhere.

Furthermore, the 5 Serpents proceeded from Right to Left. I concluded, as naively as necessary, that the Right threatened the Left, and that in 5 Months, it would kill the Left.

Now the 5 of the Serpents, $+ 6 = 11$.

11 is November.

Which gives 2. And 6 of the month and 3 of the day give 9.

And 9 is November, according to the old calendar.

And 3 of the day + 6 of the Month + 2 of the Year = 3 also, the Destruction, the Separation.

If I cover 3 with 5, I get 8, the Portal of the Infinite on earth;

which cast upon 2 of November yields 1, the Absolute Realization,

which means the Return to the Absolute,

which means the Disappearance in the Absolute,

which means the Annihilation in the Absolute and *for* the Absolute.

And if I add the 1 of the Absolute of November to the 2 of the Year of Disappearance-Destruction, I get 12: Maturity in the forms,

which means that on that day the Absolute matured in the forms and found all its forms.

And it means that *all* forms will return to the Absolute.

For it is putrefaction that ripens the Absolute today, and it is right that the year of putrefaction should have outbid the Months on that day,

Like 12 Months around 1 single Month.

Other years, other months, other days have already played with the Numbers.

But it isn't every day that we enumerate

    5 Elements

    instead of 4 Elements.

For these double Rods of Fire, where the Fire turns on itself, like the Flame around the Focus, show that the Fire will flame from the Focus,

Like the Lightning of Fiery Ether

Of which Heraclitus has already spoken.

On whatever side one turns, Destruction will be given free play everywhere.

But what do the 5 Serpents mean?

They show the 4 Elements in the midst of which Destiny will be given free play and by which it will be Returned.

A single Man has prepared them because men have deserved them.

A single man will direct them. And this man is a Tortured Man.

Here, then, is what the Tarots of June 15, 1937 revealed concerning the Tortured Man.

## DIAGRAM OF HOROSCOPE OF JUNE 15, 1937 — *on the Tortured Man*

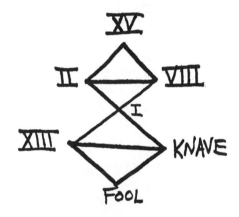

II of Pentacles: division
XV Devil: 2 principles
VIII of Pentacles: destruction
I Juggler, upsidedown: badly directed will
Knave of Batons: ruin
Fool: madness
XIII Skeleton Reaper: transformation

*Translator's Notes:* The diagram of the 3rd of June, with which these form a triangle, is missing. These two, however, are the most important for an understanding of the text. The reader will find that these two 'horoscopes' represent in the Tarots dramatical opposition, Ar-

95

# HEAVEN

TERNARY

WOMAN BEGETS ON MAN AN ABSTRACT BEING, A SPECTRAL LARVA WHICH HAS NO MORE FREE PLAY.

QUATERNARY

THE INVERTED PERVERSION OF THE WORLD HAS PRO-VOKED SERAPHISM, THE INEFFABLE WHICH APPEARS ONLY IN THE DESERTS.

A Dream of Continence has assaulted Humanity. And it is on this Abstract Dream that the World will try its fortune.

# EARTH

TERNARY

THE TORTURED MAN WAS THOUGHT A MADMAN BY THE WHOLE WORLD.

HE APPEARED AS A MADMAN BEFORE THE WHOLE WORLD.

---

taud's synthesis being completed by numerological and astrological ana-logies. This synthesis of the 2 readings is made possible by reversing the chronological order of the readings as presented in the text. The reader should know that, in the Tarots, the Batons generally represent Fire; the Swords, Air; the Pentacles, Earth; and the Cups, Water. And that, moreover, the ascending sequence XI-XIV-XVII (Spiritual Energy, Self-Mastery, Regeneration) which in the Tarots are ' reflexes ' departing from V (Abstract Man) and VIII (Justice, Portal of the In-finite), also represent paradoxically, in their sequence, the descent of the soul into matter.

AND THE IMAGE OF THE WORLD'S MADNESS IS IN-
CARNATE IN A TORTURED MAN.

QUATERNARY

THE OTHER SIDE OF THE MADMAN WAS A KING, A
DIVIDER KING PLACED AT THE SUMMIT OF THINGS,
AND HAVING ACQUIRED THE RIGHT TO DIVIDE THEM,
SAYING: THIS IS, AND THIS IS NOT.
— AND THAT WHICH WAS AND THAT WHICH WAS
NOT REMAINED FOREVER THE TWO SIDES OF REALITY,
VISIBLE AND INVISIBLE.
— HE RENDERED JUSTICE EVERYWHERE, ON ALL
LEVELS SIMULTANEOUSLY IN MOTION,
AND IT WAS AN INFERNAL JUSTICE FOR IT WAS NO
LONGER A MATTER OF RENDERING IT,

BUT OF TAKING IT AWAY.

HELL

TERNARY

NOW IT IS THE JUGGLER WHO JUDGES AND CALLS
THOSE WHO MUST BE CALLED.
HE CALLS THEM TO AN INFERNAL CONFRONTATION
IN WHICH ALL THAT PROCEEDS FROM WOMAN WILL
CONTRIBUTE TO THE DIVISION OF ALL THINGS.

QUATERNARY

THE DETACHED RECLUSE HAS AVENGED THE EVIL
THAT ISSUED FROM THE DARKNESS OF WOMAN, BY
THE POWER HE HAS JUST REINVENTED.

THE POWER HE APPLIED TO DETACHING HIMSELF HAS GIVEN HIM AN INVERSE POWER.

AND IT WAS A POWER OF DEATH.

OUR DESTINY IS A DESTINY OF DEATH. A CYCLE OF THE UNIVERSE IS FINISHED.

## CONCLUSION

Because I foresee total Destruction by Water, Earth, Fire and by a Star that shall occupy the total surface of the Air in which the Spirit of Man has bathed, I also preach total Destruction, but *Conscious and Rebellious* Destruction.

What does this mean?

It means that burning is a magic act, and that we must consent to burning, burning in advance and immediately, not a thing, but *every thing that represents things for us,* in order not to expose ourselves to being burnt up whole.

All that is not burnt by All of Us, and will not make All of Us *Madmen* and *Recluses,*

will be burnt up by the EARTH.

### A CERTAIN NUMBER OF ESSENTIAL DATES

$3 - 6 - 1937 = 11 = 2$
$15 - 6 - 1937 = \quad = 5$
$19 - 6 - 1937 = \quad = 9$

Between these three dates, which form a Triangle, the Macrocosm was illuminated. It was turned *earth-side.*

They culminate in the *Construction* of Abstract Man.

$25 - 7 - 1937 = 7$
$7 - 9 - 1937 = 9$
$3 - 11 - 1937 = 11 = 2$
$7 - 11 - 1937 = 2$

On July 25, 1937, the Macrocosm touched Earth.

On the 7th the Portal of the Infinite is opened for man. The Tortured man is at last prepared. He can enter, he stands on his own feet before his work. He can begin.

On November 3rd, Destruction is illuminated.

On the 7th, it explodes in lightning.

The Tortured Man has come at last to be Recognized by the whole world, as

## THE REVEALED

*Translated by David Rattray*

# Part II

## REVOLT AGAINST POETRY

We have never written anything except against a backdrop of the incarnation of the soul, but the soul already is made (and not by ourselves) when we enter into poetry. The poet, who writes, addresses himself to the Word, and the Word to its laws. It is in the unconscious of the poet to believe automatically in these laws. He believes himself free thereby, but he is not. There is something back of his head and over the ears of his thought. Something budding in the nape of his neck, rooted there from even before his beginning. He is the son of his works, perhaps, but his works are not of him; for whatever is of himself in his poetry has not been expressed by him but rather by that unconscious producer of life, who has pointed life out to him in order that he not be his own poet, in order that he not designate life himself; and who obviously has never been well-disposed toward him. Well, I don't want to be the poet of my poet, of that self which fancied it'd choose me to be a poet; but rather a poet-creator, in rebellion against the ego and the self. And I call to mind the old rebellion against the forms that came over me. It is by revolt against the ego and the self that I disemburden myself from all the evil incarnations of the Word, which have never been anything more for man than a compromise between cowardice and illusion, and I only know abject fornication when it comes to cowardice and illusion. And I don't want a word of mine coming from I don't know what astral libido completely aware of the formations of, say, a desire that is mine and mine alone. There is in the forms of the human Word I don't know what operation of rapaciousness, what self-devouring greed going on; whereby the poet, binding himself to the object, sees himself eaten by it. That is a crime weighing heavy on the idea of the Word-made-flesh, but the real crime is in having allowed the idea in the first place. Libido is animal-thought, and it was these same animals which one day were changed into men. The word produced through these men is the idea of an invert buried by his animal response to things, who has forgotten (through the martyrdom of time and things) that the word has been invented. The invert is he who eats his self, and desires that his self nourish him, seeking his mother in it and wanting to possess her for himself. The primitive crime of incest is the enemy of poetry and the killer of poetry's immaculacy. I don't want to eat my poem but I want to give my heart to my poem. And what is my heart to my poem? My heart is what isn't my ego. To give one's self to one's poem is also to risk being violated by it. And if I am Virgin for my poem, it ought to be virgin for my ego. I am that forgotten poet who one day saw himself hurtle to matter, and matter never will devour me, my ego. I don't want those old reflexes, results of an ancient incest come from an animal ignorance of the Virgin law of life. The ego and the self are those catastrophic states of being in which the Living Man allows himself to be imprisoned by the forms that he perceived by himself. To love his ego is to love death, and the law of the Virgin is infinite. The unconscious producer of our selves is that of an ancient copulator who frees himself to commit more vulgar magicks, and who has pulled off the most infamous wizardry by having brought himself back to his self-same self over and above his very self, eternally, so that he was able even to pull a word out of a cadaver. The libido is the definition of that cadaverous desire, and the falling man an invert criminal. I am such a primitive, discontented with the inexpiable horror of things. I don't want to reproduce myself in things but I want things to happen through my self. I don't want an idea of my ego in my poem and I don't want to meet my self again there, either. My heart is that eternal Rose come from the magic power of the initial Cross. He who crucified Himself never returned to himself. Never. For he also surrendered to Life the self by which he sacrificed Himself, after having forced it within himself to become the being of his own life. I want only to be such a poet forever, who sacrificed himself in the Kabbala of self for the immaculate conception of things.

*Translated by Jack Hirschman*

101

Artaud the actor, about 1920

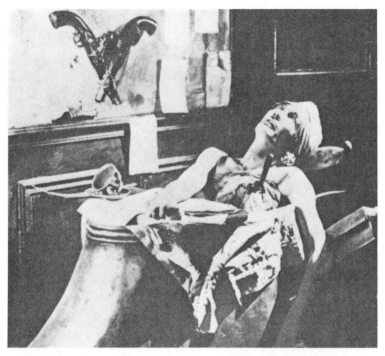

*The Dead Marat,* played by Artaud, in film, *Napoleon* (1926)

Artaud, about 1920

Artaud, about 1920

Artaud, by Balthus, about 1930

Artaud, by André Masson (1925)

# TO ADOLPH HITLER*

in memory of the
*Romanische* cafe in
Berlin one afternoon in
May of '32,
and because I pray
God
    give you the
grace to remember
all the wonders
by which HE (sic)
has GRATIFIED (RESUSCITATED)
                YOUR HEART
this very day

      Kudar dayro Zarish Ankkara
      Thabi

3 December 1943

               *Translated by Jack Hirschman*

* Editor's Note: In the December 1959 issue of *La Tour de Feu* Dr. Gaston Ferdière, Artaud's doctor at Rodez, published an article entitled ' I Treated Antonin Artaud ' in which appears the following note: ' . . . I add here a specific example of Artaud's mental derangement, the dedication to the Führer of *The New Revelations of Being* . . . One recognizes here the faulty memory (so frequent with Artaud along with mistaken identity), mystical ideas, glossolalia, etc. . . . ' This is typical psychiatric interpretation. A simpler, less ' demented ' explanation is that Artaud, rereading the *New Revelations* in Rodez, some six years after Editions Denoël had first published it, saw a connection between his prophecies and the War, and so re-dedicated his work to the man who dominated Europe the same years Artaud spent in madhouses.

# SHIT TO THE SPIRIT

After romanticism,
          symbolism,
          dadaism,
          surrealism,
          lettrism,
     and marxism,
i.e., a hundred 'schools' of political, philosophical or literary
subversion, there is one word, one thing that remains standing,
     one value that hasn't budged,
     that's kept its ancient pre-eminence through thick and thin,
     and that word and thing is spirit,
     the value attached to spirit,
     the value of the spiritual thing;
     as if it sufficed by statement
     to make that magnetic word stand out on a corner of the page,
so that everything truly were said.
     As if it were understood in fact and as principle and essence
     that spirit is the innate term,
     the model value,
          the apex word
by which the old atavistic automatism of the beast named man
might get going without jamming at the start.
     For the universal shaft would be well greased.
     It has been understood everywhere, for I don't know how many
centuries of Kabbala, hermeticism, mystagogy, platonism and psycho-
surgery,
     that the body is the son of the spirit,
     that it belongs to it like a density, a conglomeration
          or a magic mass,
     and that one cannot conceive of body as ever being, in terms of
its inborn way, the materialization of some somber marriage between
the spirit and its own power, the terminus of an elite journey of the
spirit along its own road,

*lo kundam*
*a papa*
*da mama*
*la mamama*
*a papa*
*dama*

*lokin*
*a kata*
*repara*
*o leptura*
*o ema*
*lema*

*o ersti*
*o popo*
*erstura*

*o erstura*
*o popo*
*dima*

as if it were impossible to have body without having had some part spirit; as if the state called body, the bodily thing, were in essence and by nature inferior to the spiritual state,

and came from the spiritual state.

As if the body were the carriage and the spirit the mind, which was led by another spirit, called the coachman.

As if the body were the millworkers and the spirit the boss who'd contrived how to keep them in chains.

As if the body were the body of all the soldiers who get themselves killed at the command of that great spirit, the general who makes them kill.

As if it were understood for life that the body is this filthy stuff the spirit takes its footbaths in

when there aren't bloodbaths enough for jackbooted capucine

monks to kick around in.

And the body can do nothing but buckle up.

And I'd like to see the body of a spirit in the midst of putting its future piles of flesh in order.

But before that I'd like to speak of nightmares.

Screwy jumping from one thing to another, no?

To go suddenly and brutally like that from the spirit to nightmares.

Nightmares come from all the bastards, all the body-born who are at the same time bloated with spirit, and who make magic in order to live, and who've only lived off the spirit, i.e., of magic.

Without partisans of pure spirit, of pure spirit as the origin of things, and of god as pure spirit, there never would have been any nightmares.

And everyone, of course, somewhere in the earth, blames the nightmare, accuses it of being the torturer of his last night (upon waking up), but without attaching other significance to it, without noting the gravity of the fact.

He doesn't know that the nightmare is the introduction of unreason by way of the void, is the anarchy in the inherent and normal logic of the brain, is the poison put into its well-being, is an intervention from top to bottom,

a drop of a hatred of others flowing into the breath of the night,
the instilling of a grub of spirit, a tear of pure spirit,
insinuately into the body without a sound,
by everything that is impotence, emptiness, void, hatred, frailty, envy.

Now for most sleepers on earth the nightmare is only a pretty story to tell as you jump out of bed. Something like a tale by Edgar Poe or Herman Melville or Hoffman or La Motte-Fouquet or Nathaniel Hawthorne or Lewis or Chamisso; wherein the dream furnishes the contents for the illustration of life, so to speak. But what they didn't suspect, what they don't think of telling themselves is that some people look to a nightmare

as a way of stopping life,
as a way of *their*

                    procuring
                    life
at the expense of the agony of the sleeper attacked by them.

How?

By profitting from man's sleep, from that release that sleep gives to man, in order to root out from the normal course of the molecular states of man's life a little slice of that life, a small bloody network of atoms that might serve to nourish *their* life.

A nightmare never is an accident, but an evil fastened on to us by a whore, by the mouth of a ghoul of a whore who finds us too rich with life, and so creates by very exact slurps some interferences in our thought, some catastrophic voids in the passage of the breath of our sleeping body, which believes itself free from care.

Now those who create these nightmares are men, but they are likewise spirits, spirits that wanted to stay . . . in that spiritual state, without going deeper into life.

And just what is spirit?

Spirit *in fact.*

I mean, outside philosophy.

And why would the body come from the spirit, and not vice-versa?

Why should the spirit hold all the values, while the body is only the vestment, a miserable shambles, the stuff of incarnation?

As if there had ever been a mystery called incarnation.

What connection is there between body and spirit?

Think about it awhile. There isn't any.

For we know what the body is,

but who says

that the spirit is the principle from which all that is living gushes?

It is the spirit that holds the data; it is in the spirit you see ideas.

Those womby udders bloating everything that shows energy.

But, Plato, you make us shit; and so do you, Socrates, Epictetes, Epicurus; and you, Kant, and you, Descartes, too.

For one can very well invert the problem and say that the spirit and its values and data might never have existed if the body, which at least sweated them out, had not been there, when the spirit, which never moves, was contented just to sit around and look at them,

waiting for the best one to blow;

for without the principle of sodomy there was nothing left for the spirit but to vacate the earth as well as the vast emptiness of the spheres that Plato, sad old beginner that he was, believed one day he'd furnish with ideas.

Only nobody bumped into them.

So it's all a bravado and a bluff.

A kind of smoky grub that lives only on what it has pulled from the body that was struggling to make some gesture

and not some idea or proposition.

For what, after all, are these ideas, data, values, qualities?

Terms without life that take on substance only when the body has sweated them out, going through a dead sweat in order to help them decide to let themselves go.

For the body doesn't ever need us to define what it's done.

Without the labor-pain of the body one day, an idea never would have been born,

and it isn't from the body that it was born, but against it,

when the idea of a gesture,

i.e., the shadow of it,

chose to live its own life.

Under the action already called: spirit.

That grub of expulsed wind that wanted to give itself substance without taking the trouble to earn it.

When one has no body, and therefore is nothing; when one hasn't even begun breathing, there has to be a terrible will at work in order to manufacture oneself into a something, and earn the place where breathing can go on freely.

And it isn't a matter involving an idea but rather of surmounting terrifying pangs.

And it was right there that the big bully, the big coward, that buggerer of the tide of pure essences, was knocked out; the same one who, in so far as principles and essences are concerned, and

110

without the body to resist such notions, is only a hole for the eternal passage of every idea or datum of existence, god, pure spirit, shadow and virtuality.

Too cowardly to try making it to a body, the spirits, those volatile farts more frivolous than any suffering body, roam around in the empyrean where their emptiness, their nuls and voids, their downright laziness keeps them spiritual.

By virtue of having seen the body of man underneath them, they came to the conclusion that they were going to be superior to the body of man.

By virtue of being held contemptible and repulsive by man, they've sought to give that void which is known as the spiritual state — that castration of the body of the fathermother, that impotence in slicing through anything that has life or energy — a kind of risky dignity which they've propped up by the most filthy kind of magic.

The spirit was never anything but the parasite of man, the ringworm of his worthy body when the body was no more than an animalcule swimming around and having no desire about having to be worthy of existing.

But how, by what filthy trickery, did it one day decide to be god?

That is the never-revealed story.

And I say: shit to the spirit.

I know too well by the effect of what grubby orgies, the spirit has ended up by grabbing the place before the body that actually preceded it.

I know too well that what one calls spirit is only a grinding shortage of existence, which was disgusted at the idea of becoming a body itself, and counted on what the body would lose in life in order to insure its seizure and its own subsistence

via the body that it vampirized.

The body that works has no time for thinking or, as they say, making up ideas.

Ideas are only the voids of the body. Those interferences of absence and want between two movements of a brilliant reality that the body, by its singular presence, has never stopped thrusting forward.

111

It isn't merely that matter is animated prior to thought;

it's simply that matter did not animate itself at all,

that it never went in the direction where animate perception trips along,

where either dialectic or discursive life has been able to be expressed; where culture has been able to get started;

but rather it's that body has always existed, I say body, and its manner of life or existence never had anything to do with

not only what is called spirit or idea,

but what we call the soul.

The body is a fact which dispenses with idea and all feeling emotion,

but which, from the depths of its dark cavern, throws up a look so that even the heart hasn't time quick enough to register its own existence.

Which means that when I see Claudel calling upon the spirits at the outset of the century for help, I am still able to get up a chuckle,

but when I see the word spirit in Karl Marx or Lenin,

like an old invariable value, a reminder of that eternal entity back to which all things are brought,

I tell myself that there's scum and crud abroad and god's sucked Lenin's ass:

and that's the way it's always been,

and it isn't worth talking about anymore,

it doesn't matter, it's just another fucking bill to pay.

*Translated by Jack Hirschman*

# LETTER AGAINST THE KABBALA

*Ivry*
*June 4, 1947*

My dear friend Jacques Prevel, I think I have taken about as much shit as I'm going to from Kafka, his arsoteric allegorical symbolism, as well as this Judaism of his, which contains, in the bud and on a small scale, every last one of those chicken-livered suckaprickadickadildoes that have never ceased giving me a pain in the ass for all these 10 years I have been hearing about them. They will, however, stop giving me a pain in the ass right now, because I am not about to hear another word of them, ever.

What I especially abhor in Kafka is that return of the old kike spirit (and its Christian alias), that intolerable kike mentality that hit on us first with the Kabbala and then laid on the Book of Genesis.

I doubt the world has ever known a more obnoxious crock of silly shit and sanious monkeyshines than the cock-and-ball stew known as the Kabbala, this larva coming out all over in an angry rash of the rejected angels of the mind. These rejects never made it as angels and never were a mind.

If God is above all innumerable and unfathomable, and nobody ever could or did have God's number, then why not cease and desist from incessantly measuring and enumerating all these shadows of non-being into which, according to the Kabbala, he is in the process of withdrawing, beyond any possible return or recourse, from the innumerable numbers of creation.

For what is this creation, after all (creation of what, from where, in what, of whom, by whom, toward whom and what)?

By a certain gentleman who created things while abandoning them, so as to withdraw into the center of himself, in order to make room for them and let them take care of themselves, to arise without him and against him, endlessly from the beginning to an end which (things being as the Kabbala claims they are) could never come back anyhow.

113

And out of what, whence and when are they supposed to have begun anyhow?

Why in the year 1 instead of the year zip? And is this so-called year 1 the ONE of our era, instead of the preceding one; and, if so, whence, when and since when?

God does not exist, he withdraws, gets the fuck on out and leaves the cops to keep an eye on things. He separates from himself 3 cops divided into 3. Okay, but why not 4 or 2 or 1 or zero or nothing at all? And from where did these 3 incorrigibly filthy accomplices of the father, the son, the holy ghost (the father, mother and son), come to equal 1 and not 3?

After all this, it should be obvious to anyone that the Kabbala was a simple book, simple in the sense of simpleton, but written by those who were simple not in spirit or of spirit, but in and of virtues, and who never had any other virtue than that of being simple, i.e., in the plainest and most simple concrete sense: assholes.

What is this number 3 they keep harping on like some revelation of the secrets of the universal cipherable quantity forever rattling on like an egg-checker in a henhouse? So the hen laid the egg in 3 days. So what!

When a man holds his preconceived offspring on the pink tip of his cock, he and his wife equal 2 and only 2; the number 3 is still a virtuality in space, and a virtuality that can quite easily be aborted.

And then where is the triad? The threefold scheme of this erotic egg-checker by which this third term has not yet been devoured?

And who can say whether it would ever be devoured, if twins came out instead of one?

What happens then to the threefold scheme of this universally predestined triad? I too once had a vision of the countenance, that famous countenance which beheld not the countenance; but this primordial countenance was no countenance at all, but rather a huge asshole; for the asshole not the countenance is the cavity out of which all the things of this world here below have issued.

To be continued in the next issue. . . .

ANTONIN ARTAUD

P.S., The truth of the matter is entirely different from what the Kabbala claims to expound transcendentally.

The world was left to mankind not as a creation but as a reject, a foul-smelling turd that the Ancient of Days withdrew from when he made zimzum, not in order to make room for it but because he just didn't want to risk touching it with a ten-foot pole.

A horrible turd trembling expectantly in the void, on the verge of the still uncreated man, exploded;

and the uncreated man (sardonically known in the Kabbala as the old Adam) jumped up with a start,

jumped into himself, all by himself, and

all the way up to

himself,

beyond the void that was staring him in the face, encompassing him like a crushingly everpresent and insatiable need, as we are told in the books of hermetic scholarship used by the forever insatiable ignorance of the so-called ' Initiates.'

The truth of the matter is simply that this man was too clean and jumped back and shrank from it as from the stink of a fart or some other filth representing the created world.

Which was, at the worst, nothing more than the accident of a genesis by perpetual gestation; for the world is never finished; and it was from this accident that the base cowardice of the rabbis dragged out the primary series a, b, c, d, which they indefatigably and by kabbalistic reduction brought back to the prime numbers 1, 2, 3, in the *Zohar* and the *Sepher Yetzirah*.

And why did it all have to happen on that particular day and not on any other day;

why did there have to be a beginning of things,

beginning at that precise moment and regarding that particular world?

Why a world made in just that way,

I mean that stupidly,

a world of a, b, c, of arithmetic and alphabet;

why couldn't it have been some world without numbers or letters and made exclusively for illiterates who never knew how to count?

> yam camdou
> yan daba
> camdoura
> yan camdoura
> a daba roudou

Is there anyone who can't see that it is just this (by now inveterate) framework of numbers and letters which has at last asphyxiated and ancestrally damned mankind?

To what advantage and whose profit, by virtue of whom and what? And that is why we are today confronted with a humanity in such an advanced state of syphilization, it cannot perceive that it is this very grammatical method that has made a scourge of all the so-called great ideas of civilization and culture that man himself bends to, as to an iron yoke which prevents him from advancing.

Civilization is here
and culture there.

As for your way of thinking about them, man, it will always have to be grammatical, numerical, symmetrical, arithmetical, acoustical or not at all.

Which means that science, taken as the genital repository of all elements permitting life and being, is in the hands of a certain number of Jack-offs, a very select party which, in addition, shits all over any other parties who may not measure up to their particular and sectarian way of thinking; and who started off by locking arms and holding hands and electing themselves as a very select party, and established this somber group which (though nobody any longer knows, or can even yet suspect, this) is at the bottom not only of all wars, all famines, all restrictions of nourishment, all revolutions and all anarchies, but also of all epidemics, of all physiological deficiencies, of the born man, of all dietary scurvies, of all spontaneous generations of deaf-mutes, and of those born blind, mongoloid idiots and incarnate morons who often have nothing wrong with them other than a certain excess of dermis and epidermis by which their wires get crossed and their mental electricity cannot properly be grounded;

and it is always on the Kabbala, be it as it may, on the *Zohar,* the *Sepher Yetzirah,* the *Vedas,* the *Upanishads,* the *Puranas,* and the *Ramayana,* that this unknown and somber group bases the continuing persistence of its misdeeds.


We are an unkempt humanity
led by a small but tireless
kennel of initiates.

For these 4 or five apparently benign books, which are actually the 4 or five chief and major psychic (and I mean psychic) emotive crimes against humanity, are used by this group of initiates as leverage to turn the screw, tighten the strangle-knot, and hold dangling in the framework of its notations (which were never denounced by anyone before me), to hold, I say, and dangle in this strangle-hold the anatomical breath of life, now so rare and deficient in a humanity they have with such deliberate care infected, polluted, sodomized and scrupulously syphilized.

Let man make love at a loss, say the initiates of arithmetic and grammar; meanwhile, we will continue to hold the reins of a power that never could exist except in the parasitical proliferation of the act known as orgasm, coitus, copulation, fornication;

which amounts to making man into a sucker for a big infected piece of communion-wafer candy on a stick, a regular all-day sucker, so they could keep a hold not only on man himself but even on that certain something more, which has been called the divinity of man.

Yes, by using a routine that involved grammar, arithmetic, Zohar, Vedas, Upanishads, Puranas and other Kabbalas, these initiates have managed to keep their hold on that whole complex of the inveterate fetishes of mankind, which has been called the occult steps of divinity.

Thus syphilized in a framework of grammar and number, man still manages to stand upright by dint of coitus and orgasm, in the midst of wars, epidemics, famines, blackmarkets and other treacheries by which he has from time immemorial sealed his compact in letters of

117

blood on a dark parchment of scrotums and foreskins ( I say foreskins) clipped from each pink and rabid tip frothing and dripping with the mongrel scum of this physiological and kabbalistical kennel of initiates.

I mean that the masters of man, who inspired in him the Kabbala and its primary numbers, are themselves certain lost elements of a humanity in full flower, which betrayed its august form —

which was nonformalized

and fathomed —

for a handy grammatical form, because it did not wish to take the trouble of counting higher than

1, 2 and 3.


*Saturday, the Eve of the Pentecost*
*8:25 p.m.*
regarding the *Zohar*,
the *Sepher Ha-Zohar*,
which,
in its affirmative smugness,
in its so-called transcendant and
primal hermeticism, is
the most crassly idiotic book
ever written,
and they know it,
know it is the *Zohar* by virtue of nothing
but the pen that wrote it:
the inept rabbis who thought they were old hands at the angel game when they wrote it in that angelic state, and — given this feeling — would have done better to go get their asses reamed and diddled than to slobber their scholarly boners of Genesis, which any six-year-old child would have brains enough to dismember, and never have to remember the abc of those misers, who were as arbitrary as they were fixed.

The famous *Zohar* teaches us
nothing,
it establishes nothing,

sets forth nothing,
advances nothing,
announces nothing,
recalls nothing,
calls up nothing,
is not poetic,
offers as its harmony nothing
but a little amateur harmonizing of moldy
burial vaults,
just a little harmonizing for mildewed
religious skeletons,
which a true man feels every minute like
smashing,
but isn't even impelled to that because
it isn't even stiff enough to smash,
better just to kick aside, that decrepit
and anachronistic harmony.
Things do not come out of the
triad.
They do not come out of the number one,
or the monad
          either.
Neither do they come from
the o, the zero
          beneath one
          on top of one
          or without one:
they come from nothing at all.
And, besides, they don't come.
They haven't got here yet.
This is why the *Zohar* is an anachronistic
book:
          out of all line
          or sequence,
which teaches nothing and can reveal nothing to anybody about a

truth
which doesn't even exist
because it *is* not yet
arisen
and, moreover, it never will
arise.
It's all an academic game for apprentice
sorcerers.
Tau for ticktacktoe.


As for explaining their Genesis, it could have been done otherwise than by this arch-conventional scheme of tallying by three, which anyway was outdated ever since it was thought of.

The number 3
is just as idiotic as the sign of the
cross.
The pair of them were well-designed
to go together;
as well as the threadbare sophistry of the trinity of the father, the son and the innumerable ghost
which the magnetic dial of a
cross
designed for a world which, without it,
would not exist:
an erotic world that swoons and burns,
a world that swells and froths
at the teats,
a world that revived death by sperm,
which was on the way out
when the cross crossed its path
and crossed it out
so that, ever since, the world has been
hung-up (crucified)

arrested.

No pigfoot is more grandiose than the semitic symbol of the cruciform insemination of this (urethral, urinary) cosmos,

the issue of funerary sperm of

thought,

which the Saint, the Master, the Man

had condemned and deplored,

and which the men of death, (the spectres of existence, the beings) amassed in order to be reborn because they were dead.

And we are in the world of the dead, which is the hell into which Man has recently descended, and where he dwells among all the legions of the damned;

and this is the truth.

The *Zohar* is a book of the damned, made and written by the damned while awaiting a

corporeal,

definitive

punishment which should not be much longer in arriving.

This is why it could never teach, reveal, explain anything — being, as it was, the ignorant residue of an assembly of ignorant brains,

who wrote out of memories, *framed by them* into an ideal diagram, of a world that had rejected them.

Such beings born by nature cannot understand the infinite without number, and need to submit it, in order to understand it, to the most elementary possible system of enumeration; and so they chose the number 3 as the one that seemed closest to their own born barnyard rhythm.

It should be noted that 3 with a

brain of genius,

and on the forehead of an authentic being

of genius,

would have been able to enter into the

mystery,

to grow this number of its own

*innate*

mystery,

appearing as a sort of bewitchment, an entity too deep-rooted ever
to be extirpated; thus
when everything was nothing
and 3 cried out in the deserts of infinity for a gathering together
by 3,
the angular accumulation of the triad
of beings,
which by 2's could not stand at an angle
and by 4's was clustered together,
reassembling and piling in again,
made what one might call an angular redistribution
of the 2
into the 3 which, for that reason, is innumerable;
but that is a reason the *Zohar* never gave, a reason it never even
hinted at,
and all it did was baaa

> about the isolation
> and the reduction
> of a one,

I say, grotesquely,

> of a one,
> of the imperceptible
> and inaccessible
> one
> in three,

pederastically, in the beginning, father,
son and ghost,
not the family
father, mother and

> baby wee.

When confronted with the bilge gargle of the gurgling swill of

> this blood-curdling
> and garbled inspiration
> that impregnates me,

I feel the umbilical belly of my testicles bulge with a future and

immediate spawn
> *that will be born.*

Which means that the erotic appetite of Satan's hot bellows are blowing me in and out, by an ingrown coitus.

This, without Zohar, is the simple physiological explanation.

There is yet another, which Hermes, double of god, can now corroborate:

it is that

the universal body, weary of being wrongly and uselessly blown up and out of shape, pulls itself together in a kind of immeasurable hunger for life,

which trembles at the monotonous and never-ceasing meanness into which forever it continues to be plunged.

*Translated by David Rattray*


# LETTER ON LAUTREAMONT

Yes, I do have some inside information for you on the unthinkable Count de Lautréamont,* on the magnetic extravagance of his letters, those dark iron-fisted dictates he sent with such elegance — cordiality, even — to his father, banker, publisher or friends. Extravagant? Of course. These letters have that harsh extravagance of a man who rushes forward with his lyricism like an erect avenging blade in one hand or the other.

Incapable of a simple everyday letter, he always gives the sense of a certain epileptoid tremor of the Word, which, for whatever object, does not lend itself to being utilized without a shudder.

This Word nurtures a single inhabitant: Poetry, swimming in the infinitesimal detail of it like a frog and, with each letter, swelling up into a bigbertha ejaculating broadsides against all that is bovine.

One letter, no two-bit note but one worth double the untouchable price of Baudelaire's and Lautréamont's poetry put together, announces to a publisher an enclosed payment in stamps — not postage stamps

* *nom de plume* of Isidore Ducasse — Ed.

123

but 'postal' stamps — for the last poems of Baudelaire. With its hollow humor, insistent though surreptitious, the word *postal* lays bare to the bone those stiff little pictures by means of which the book is to be paid for; *postal*: a splinter under the fingernail, mere sliver of an idea, pedalpoint skipping in the dark beneath his big feet. Which, if the reader cannot understand, then the reader is nothing but a hog stuffed mollycoddled faggot.

Something like that totem-hole of bestiality forever seated on its ass (and the idea of beauty has been thus seated for a long time, according to Arthur Rimbaud). Such a beast would keep, between its impure thighs, those thirty silver pieces that were to be the poet's, not for unfinished and unwritten poems, but for that bleeding incarnadine pouch which the night ceaselessly beats, and which goes, then, like every bourgeois, for a stroll. That pouch of leaping influxes which, in the chest of a great poet, does not beat the same way as it does elsewhere; for it's right here that every bourgeois battens, on this heart which strictly, stubbornly, jealously, aggressively has ever kept rigid and holding to its own, bone-hard in its resistance to coercion. For the contemptuous and hypocritical citizen, sedate and sedative, potbelly stuffed with contempt and certitude, is nothing really but that greedy antiquity of a monkey, that ancient Ramayana monkey, that antique pickpocket sneaking up on every pulsation of instant poetry, the instant it goes off. ' Oh but such things aren't done, no, of course such things just aren't done,' he says to the Count de Lautréamont. We ought to turn a deaf ear to such things (and by ' ear ' is meant this cavern of the anus where every bourgeois, well-stuffed and barded with *anti-strophe,* is a pickpocket of poetry). Stop. Get back in line, be normal.

Your heart pounds with horror, but that is not seen. And as for me, I also have a meat heart that's always in need of you. What do you mean? None of your business.

But Lautréamont will not be stopped. ' Permit me,' he says to his publisher, ' to start on a slightly upstage note.' The slightly upstage note of his death, no doubt, which made away with him one off-color day. For there has never been quite enough attention, and, I insist, *remorse* expended on the death, so trite and yet so evasive, of this unthinkable Count de Lautréamont.

This death was too trite, too anodyne, not to arouse a desire to examine more closely the mystery of his life. For, after all, just what did the poor Isidore Ducasse die of, who was no doubt a genius irreducible to the world and no more desirable to the world than Edgar Poe, Baudelaire, Gérard de Nerval or Arthur Rimbaud.

Did he die of a long or a short ailment? Was he found deceased in bed at sun-up? What history has to say is simple, simple and sinister: the coroner's certificate was signed by the hotel manager and the bellhop who happened to be on duty.

For a great poet this seems a bit short, a bit meager, and in fact there is something in it so sly, so evasively offhand and sly that in certain spots it fairly stinks with meanness, and the furtive vulgar matter-of-factness of his burial just does not agree with the life of Isidore Ducasse; although to my mind it agrees only too well with all the monkey business of that surreptitiousness of hatred by which the pickpoet stupidity of the middleclass will fuck over any great name.

But who was that unwashed dumb slut I heard one day telling me that if the Count de Lautréamont hadn't died at twenty-four, at the beginning of his existence, he too would have had to be *put away* like Nietzsche, Van Gogh, or the unfortunate Gérard de Nerval.

For if the Maldoror pose is acceptable in a book, it is acceptable only after the poet's death — maybe a hundred years later — when the astringent explosives of the poet's virid heart have had time to calm down. For as long as he is alive, they are too powerful. In like manner, they had to shut up Baudelaire, Edgar Poe, Gérard de Nerval, and the unthinkable Count de Lautréamont. Because they were afraid that their poetry might leap out of the books and turn reality upsidedown . . . and so they shut up Lautréamont when he was still young in order immediately to be done with that increasing aggressiveness of a heart that was catastrophically sickened by everyday life and would have in the long run succeeded in sweeping away on every side the unbelievable cynical jesuitical cunning of its indefatigable tortures.

'Having got past the red light,' says poor Isidore Ducasse, 'she permits him, for a modest fee, to scrutinize the interior of her cunt.'

It is no great news that this sentence can be found in the *Chants de Maldoror*, and it is no news, either, that it should be there, for the whole book consists of nothing but hideous sentences of this sort. Yes, in the *Chants de Maldoror*, everything is hideous: the legs of an unfortunate woman trying to bring on an abortion, or a last bus going out. Everything is like that sentence where the Count de Lautréamont (or rather I think it was poor Isidore Ducasse and not the unthinkable Count de Lautréamont) sees a stick coming through the closed venetian blinds of a room in the most sinister crib (*crib*: vulgar slang for *good-time* or *cathouse*) and is told by this stick that he is not a stick at all but a hair fallen from the head of his master, some munificent dude whose money gave him the right to flay a miserable woman in the epidermis of a pair of sheets, clean maybe to start with, but nauseous afterwards.

And I say that there was within Isidore Ducasse a spirit that forever wanted to drop Isidore Ducasse in favor of the unthinkable Count de Lautréamont, a very fine name, a very great name. And I say that the invention of the name Lautréamont, even if it did serve Isidore Ducasse as a password to protect and introduce the unheard-of magnificence of his product; I say that the invention of this literary patronymn, like a costume masking life, gave rise, by masking the man who had produced it, to one of those collective jobs of dirty work that fill the history of letters, and at last made the soul of Isidore Ducasse flee from life. For it was Isidore Ducasse who died and not the Count de Lautréamont, and it was Isidore Ducasse who gave the Count de Lautréamont something to survive on, and there is little to prevent me, I should even say nothing to prevent me from supposing that this impersonal unthinkable Count of the coat-of-arms Lautréamont was a sort of undefinable murderer staring Isidore Ducasse straight in the eye.

And I think it is this and nothing else that, in the last analysis, on that last day, poor Isidore Ducasse died of; though in history, the Count de Lautréamont was to survive him. For it was none other than Isidore Ducasse who invented the name Lautréamont. But when he invented it, he was not alone. I mean that around him and his soul there were sprouting that germ-infested tuft of espionage, that acrimonious slobbering throng of the most sordid parasites of being, all the motheaten antique spectres of non-being, and a shower of innate scabs and profiteers who whispered to him on his deathbed: 'We're the Count de Lautréamont, and you're nothing but Isidore Ducasse, and if you won't admit that you're only Ducasse and we're Lautréamont, the author of the *Chants de Maldoror*, we'll kill you.' And so he died one little dawn, this side of an impossible night. Sweating, staring at his death as if through the orifice of his coffin, poor no-'count Isidore Ducasse at the feet of the rich Count de Lautréamont.

And this is not called an uprising of chattel against the master, but an orgy of the collective unconscious trespassing on individual consciousness.

One point I insist on is that Isidore Ducasse was neither madman nor visionary, but a genius who never ceased as long as he lived to see with perfect lucidity when he observed and poked around in the fallow and yet unploughed furrows of the unconscious. His own, that is, and nobody else's; for there are no points in our body where we can commune with a collective consciousness. We are alone, all alone, in our body. But the world has never admitted this and it has always wished to retain for itself some means of scrutinizing more closely the consciousness of all great poets, and everybody wants to get inside everybody else's mind so as to know what everybody else is up to.

And one day certain persons, not highborn kinsmen, as in Edgar Poe's 'Annabel Lee,' but mean scabs of being, the itch of all that is eaten up with envy, came whispering to Isidore Ducasse up alongside his bed and his head and at the head of his deathbed: 'You are a genius, but I am the genius that inspires your consciousness, and it is I who write your poems inside you, before you even think of them, and better than you ever could.' And so it was that Isidore Ducasse died of rage for having wished, like Edgar Poe, Nietzsche, Baudelaire and Gérard de Nerval, to preserve his intrinsic individuality instead of becoming like Victor Hugo, Lamartine, Musset, Blaise Pascal or Chateaubriand, the funnel of everybody's thoughts.

For the operation does not consist of sacrificing one's ego as a poet at the moment one is *alienated* from everybody, but it consists of letting oneself be penetrated and raped by collective consciousness in such a way, that one is no longer in one's own body anything but a slave to the ideas and reactions of all others.

And the name Lautréamont was only a first step of which Isidore Ducasse was not, perhaps, wary enough — a first step towards perverting in favor of the collective consciousness the arch-individual works of Isidore Ducasse, poet enraged by truth.

I mean to say that in the limbo of death where he now is, other consciousnesses and other egos than his own are doubtless at this very moment obscenely screaming for joy to think that they took part in the creative emulsion of his poems and of his shrieks, and are getting some kind of obscure kicks at the very thought of enraging this poet in order to suffocate and kill him.

*Translated by David Rattray*

# COLERIDGE THE TRAITOR

My soul (today I have no more soul, and I've never believed in its existence) is always tending to go black. Going there as an ignoramus, for I am a perfect innocent.

That's why you were right to ask me for something on Coleridge. Not that I think Coleridge enters into that current of damned poets, of outcasts capable of *transpiring* at a given moment, of ejecting that little black mucous, that waxy fart of hideous pain at the end of the turnstile of blood, which Baudelaire (or his real aphasia), Edgar Poe, Gérard de Nerval, and perhaps Villon let go of at the ultimate point of horror. As for Lautréamont I believe that the fart belongs to Isidore Ducasse, and the turnstile to Lautréamont. I say Lautréamont *second*; for it's because he, Isidore Ducasse, desired to be the Count of Lautréamont that he died.

And for Coleridge also the question of being poses itself, and of communicating what he realized he was, and it's because he wanted to say it *completely* that he died. I say died also between the age of twenty and twenty-four, and that Samuel Taylor Coleridge, who prepared himself to outclass Dante, is known for nothing more than being the author of ' The Rhyme of the Ancient Mariner,' ' Christabel,' and ' Kubla Khan.' And some will say that that's better than nothing, and that it signifies one of the great poets of the English language. Perhaps. But so much the worse for the English language; for it's also true that that same English *tongue* had given to the obvious, authentic and intrinsic heart of Samuel Taylor Coleridge, which was *panting,* one of those turns of the meat-grinder, one of those dirty turns that meat tongues never are able to abstain from giving to the heart of poets coming to birth, I mean that Mr. Satisfactory Sex, in complicity with Mrs. Erotic Orgasm, rose up one day against the poet about to be born,

and, by a twist of the tongue, made him turn and drift from himself, and come full-circle back,

for that's just the way it goes.

I mean that I've read, among the youthful poems of Samuel Taylor Coleridge, a little unfinished poem of a few lines where Samuel Taylor Coleridge takes up the old, unfinished and to a certain extent *aborted* work of Euripides, and undertakes knowingly and firmly to lash with words as if given over to idolatry, to drive the occult into his scheme, to redeem man from God, to transport the occult into the open, to do what one says, I mean what the whole mind (precisely because it is mind and not body, and precisely because it isn't life and has never been part of the living) has always pretended that it didn't have to do, which is precisely to practice occultism in public, to convey the occult world into the open in order to show clearly from what nothingness it is created.

For that which is secret gathers together and roots itself and grows dark, the more so when it is pointed out, undressed, discovered.

129

So that you have to strip the virgin down to his erection for the whore, with the two of them filthily screwing the maidenhead, drubbing it to the level of a god, after which, the place being cleaned up, the authentic body of the poet comes back, comes back belching blood, for all true poetry is cruel, it's not some sparrow — and that's the kind of thing Samuel Taylor Coleridge went through between the age of twenty and twenty-four,

after which he pulled up short.

Then he too fell prey to the buried and concealed Fable (the Fable* meaning that the whole poem is returned in time all the way back to the genesis of the myth out of which life supposedly issued,

although it's here and now,
in the immediate,
right in front of us that life issues,
and all we have to do is look at it more closely
and we will see it welling up
tumescent and black,
bitter, repulsive, gaseous
as a rough papiermaché fart,
and the genesis and the myth were created
in order only to paralyze
the poet,
and therefore to prevent him
from seeing,
from seeing that reality was in the [                    ])
and that the Fable is unreality, masked by a threefold key.

Why threefold?
And why a key?
Always it got in the way of Samuel Taylor Coleridge and his self, for there is throughout the whole story of this world I don't know

* Translator's Note: Artaud wrote ' Coleridge the Traitor ' in the form of a letter to his friend Henri Parisot, who had translated the three poems of Coleridge referred to, and had asked Artaud for a preface. Shortly before his death Artaud scribbled down some variants of the original text, written on November 17, 1946. Many of these are illegible, but I have tried working them into the original to the best advantage.

what idiotic bias for mystery, for the Key, for the *Trinity* and Holy Mother, and the Number which can no more manage to get free of numerals (which means something only to the one receptive to it), than the smothered pipe of the old mariner of Coleridge can get out of the habit of reckoning the sun by the years; and as for those years, I don't know by what kind of trinitarian gravitation enslaving humanity, this humanity still hasn't been able to raise itself to the effort of thinking, not even for one little instant per century,

and will not even now raise itself to the effort of concluding once and for all *that it hasn't found the Key.*

This being so, I can't consider ' The Rhyme of the Ancient Mariner,' ' Christabel,' and ' Kubla Khan ' as more than the remains of a senseless ruin that poetry built 150 years ago, which was caused by its having rediscovered the igneous cord, that thick hemp in the neck of the priest about to be hung, that rope which, in the midst of this drift from reality toward a distant poetical *virtuality,* of this dislocation of the true world in favor of an occult erotic reality, the more occult in that it is obscene, and the more obscene in that it is true — that rope which stands for, I say, the true villain of the misdeed, who is the priest and the INITIATE.

But that, the occult said to Samuel Taylor Coleridge, that *is what you will never tell.*

As for me, I love nothing but poetry.

Yes, and that's just the obscenity of the thing; for the middleclass tongue, the blow of the erotic tongue of Mrs. Obscene Little Middleclass, has also loved nothing but poetry.

I say real poetry, poetic poetry, *etic*: charming hiccup with a bloody red backdrop, the backdrop forced into poematic, the poematic of hemorrhaging reality. For afterwards, let's say *after* the ' poematic, will come the regime of the blood. Since *ema* in Greek means blood, so po-ema should mean

> afterwards:
> the blood,
> the blood afterwards.

First let's make a poem, with blood.

Later on we'll eat the time of the blood.

Now let's get the po-em off the ground, singing. And *without* blood. For whatever's been made with blood, we've made a poem of.

And what do you think the gregorian chant comes from, that interrupted rape of an emulsion of blood?

and what do you think certain Tibetan mantras come from?

From having desired to avoid the blood, from having forever distilled the blood, and in that blood the real truth, in order to make
what is called
*poetry*
*today,*
absence of cruelty in our time.

So go on with your overblow of modest and erotic tonguing, the modest orgasms of the middleclass.

This world of war and blackmarket: how many kids has it forced into existence each year, how many kids has it drilled into the body, into that thick lining of uterus, without ever having acknowledged the suffering or blood that it was spilling while it filthily screwed its kids,

cowardly screwed its little children.

Stay back of me, cruelty of the thing; but you, you bloodless poem, go on ahead, but singing.

So Samuel Coleridge did see clearly. He did see that the priest, the initiate, the guru, the savant, in complicity with the shopwindow quack and the yogi behind folding screens, don't stop whipping on the sly the true heart of the suffering poet in order to put a stop to the mucous of the blood.

Yes, under the tourniquet of pain, there's a blood that issues in the form of a clot given a one-hour thaw from the frigidaire of hell, and this clot is that true sexless child, born outside the slimy childbirths of the sex that was but the gullet and spike of a primitive strangulation,

— and for not having been believed when he came bearing the gift of his insane mucous, Gérard de Nerval hanged himself from a streetlamp; and for not having been able to adapt himself to his mucous, the Count de Lautréamont died of fury; and in the face of all this, what did Samuel Taylor Coleridge do?

He transformed the mucous that was taken from him into opium, and so he took laudanum till the day he died.

And under the cloak of opium he has written his poemuzeeks.

He set a ship and a crime adrift. The ship in the icebergs of the Pole, under the sun of a crime that was late-born.

For the strange thing about 'The Rhyme of the Ancient Mariner' is that crime which nothing can explain and which, upon careful reading of the poem, we see is born *after* and not *during* his thought.

And I've looked for the darkness in those three poems of Coleridge, but I've never really found it.

And one day I realized that it was that darkness, that darkness of the poem itself, Coleridge had given up on.

And that he was given a chance to regret it.

A chance to simply regret it, but on the condition that he turn it into a pretty music.

For Samuel Taylor Coleridge ended up by forgetting everything.

And in 'Kubla Khan' did his memory come back to him? I don't believe so. I believe that the cunning of the liturgical spirit, which, out of the howls of suppliants, makes rituals good enough for matinal intonation to the tune of the cock in the briskness of morning, went so far as to dress up the mortal remains of the *other* soul of Samuel Taylor Coleridge with so many phantoms, so many nullified *beings,* that even the great treasure his poem was hiding turned out to be nothing but an outdated eden, the kind belonging to all those who have given themselves to God and not to man; for it is man who is to be redeemed, who is now left with the task of redeeming himself. And Coleridge remembered a story of a spirit who lived in a state of consolation, but who lived it

*ritualized*

above humanity.

In that kind of eternal state which really is never detached from limbo,

and can never enter reality.

When Samuel Taylor Coleridge came to understanding, between the age of twenty and twenty-four, he did have an understanding of the true world.

The human earth *without mortality*.

Coleridge saw himself as immortal, and he was about to use the means of living, I mean of surviving to the point when we'd meet,

when I don't know what robed priest, what guru from Bardo, who never existed but in a sexless life, toward which he's always drawing every last one of the human dead, came and quoted him wrong on the price of mucous. He drew him toward the horrible pain that was entirely conjured up by his secular and premeditated magic, for in reality it didn't exist.

I believe that Samuel Taylor Coleridge was a weakling, that he got scared; and it may be that Samuel Taylor Coleridge also realized what he truly was.

That he wasn't *man* enough to give out with that mucous for life, for immortal life; and undoubtedly the crime of the ancient mariner is that of Coleridge himself, and the albatross is that soul of man which Coleridge killed in order to live. And I think that soon I will know all this very precisely, yes, very precisely.

*Translated by Jack Hirschman*

# VAN GOGH
# THE MAN SUICIDED BY SOCIETY

*introduction*

You can say all you want about the mental health of Van Gogh who, during his lifetime, cooked only one of his hands, and other than that did no more than cut off his left ear,

in a world in which every day they eat vagina cooked in green sauce or the genitals of a newborn child whipped into a rage

plucked as it came out of the maternal sex.

And this is not an image, but a fact abundantly and daily repeated and cultivated throughout the world.

And thus, demented as this assertion may seem, present-day life goes on in its old atmosphere of prurience, of anarchy, of disorder, of delirium, of dementia, of chronic lunacy, of bourgeois inertia, of psychic anomaly (for it isn't man but the world that has become abnormal), of deliberate dishonesty and downright hypocrisy, of a mean contempt for anything that shows breeding,

of the claim of an entire order based on the fulfillment of a primitive injustice,

in short, of organized crime.

Things are bad because the sick conscience now has a vital interest in not getting over its sickness.

So a sick society invented psychiatry to defend itself against the investigations of certain visionaries whose faculties of divination disturbed it.

Gérard de Nerval was not mad, but he was accused of being so, in order to discredit certain vital revelations he was about to make,

and besides being so accused, he was hit on the head, physically hit on the head one night, to make him forget the monstrous facts which he was going to reveal and which, by this blow, were pushed back within him, onto the supernatural plane; because all of society, secretly united against his consciousness, was at that moment strong enough to make him forget its reality.

135

No, Van Gogh was not mad, but his paintings were wildfire, atomic bombs, whose angle of vision, compared to all the other paintings popular at the time, would have been capable of upsetting the larval conformity of the Second Empire bourgeoisie, and of the yes-men of Thiers, Gambetta, Felix Faure, as well as those of Napoleon III.

For Van Gogh's painting doesn't attack a certain conformity of manners and morals, but the conformity of institutions themselves. And even Nature with its climates, tides, equinoctial storms, cannot maintain the same gravitation after Van Gogh's stay on earth.

All the more reason, on the social plane, for institutions to disintegrate, and for medicine, which resembles a stale and useless corpse, to declare Van Gogh insane.

Faced with Van Gogh's lucidity, always active, psychiatry becomes nothing but a den of gorillas, so obsessed and persecuted that it can only use a ridiculous terminology to palliate the most frightful anxiety and human suffocation

worthy product of their warped minds.

Indeed there is not a psychiatrist who is not a notorious erotomaniac.

And I don't believe that the rule of the confirmed erotomania of psychiatrists suffers a single exception.

I know of one who rebelled a few years ago, at the idea of my accusing his whole profession of being filled with low scoundrels and patented shysters.

As for me, Monsieur Artaud, he said, I'm not an erotomaniac. I challenge you to show me a single instance on which you can base your accusation.

All I need do, Dr. L . . . . is to point you out as proof.

You bear the stigma on your mug,

you dirty bastard.

You have the puss of one who inserts his sexual prey under his tongue and then turns it over like an almond, disdaining it as it were.

This is called feathering one's nest and providing for a rainy day.

If during coitus you have not been able to chuckle from the glottis in a way you know very well, to gurgle from the pharynx, the oesophagus, the urethra, and the anus at the same time, you cannot say that you are satisfied.

And through your internal organic thrill you have fallen into a rut which is the incarnate proof of your foul prurience.

You cultivate this year-in and year-out, and more and more, because socially speaking there is no law against it,

but it falls under another law where the whole injured consciousness suffers because, believing the way you do, you prevent it from breathing.

You call active consciousness delirium, while on the other hand, you strangle it with your ignoble sexuality.

And that is precisely where poor Van Gogh was chaste.

As chaste as a seraph or a virgin could never be, because they are the very ones

who fomented

and fed, in the beginning, the great machine of sin.

Furthermore, Dr. L . . . ., perhaps you belong to the race of iniquitous seraphim, but for pity's sake leave men alone.

Van Gogh's body, spared from sin, was also spared the madness that sin alone fosters.

And I do not believe in Catholic sin,

but I believe in the erotic crime from which, as it happens, all the geniuses of the earth,

the genuinely insane men in asylums, protect themselves;

otherwise, it could happen that they are not (genuinely) insane.

And what is a genuine lunatic?

He is a man who prefers to go mad, in the social sense of the word, rather than forfeit a certain higher idea of human honor.

That's how society strangled all those it wanted to get rid of, or wanted to protect itself from, and put them in asylums, because they refused to be accomplices to a kind of lofty swill.

For a lunatic is a man that society does not wish to hear but wants to prevent from uttering certain unbearable truths.

But in that case, internment is not the only weapon, and the concerted assemblage of men has other ways of undermining the wills of those it wants to break.

Aside from the trifling witchcraft of country sorcerers there are tricks of global hoodoo in which all alerted consciousnesses participate periodically.

This is why during a war, a revolution, a hatching social upheaval, the collective conscience is questioned and questions itself, and also voices its own judgement.

It can also happen that it is aroused and rises above itself in certain outstanding individual cases.

That is why there was a collective spell cast on Baudelaire, Edgar Allen Poe, Gérard de Nerval, Nietzsche, Kierkegaard, Hölderlin and Coleridge.

There was a spell cast on Van Gogh also.

It can happen during the day but preferably, and generally, it happens at night.

That is how strange forces are aroused and transported to the astral vault, to that kind of dark dome which is composed above all of human breathing and of the poisonous aggressiveness of the evil minds of most people.

That is how the few rare, well-intentioned and lucid wills that had to struggle on this earth saw themselves at certain hours of the day and night in the throes of real and waking nightmares, surrounded by formidable suction, the formidable tentacular oppression of a kind of civic magic which will soon appear undisguised.

Confronted by this concerted swill, which deals with sex on the one hand and the masses of some other psychic rites on the other as a base or point of support, there is nothing unbalanced in walking around at night with 12 candles attached to your hat to paint a landscape from nature;

how else could Van Gogh have had light, as our friend the actor Roger Blin so rightly pointed out the other day?

As for the cooked hand, that was heroism pure and simple;

as for the severed ear, that was direct logic,

and I repeat,

a world that, day and night and more and more eats the uneatable in order to bring its evil will around to its own ends,

has nothing else to do at this point
but to shut up.

## *p o s t - s c r i p t u m*

Van Gogh did not die of a condition of delirium proper
but of having bodily become the field of a problem
that the iniquitous spirit of mankind has debated since the
beginning of time,
the predominance of flesh over spirit, or body over flesh or the
mind over one or the other.

And where in this delirious thinking is there room for the human
ego?

Van Gogh searched for his during his entire lifetime, and with a
strange energy and determination.

And he did not commit suicide in a fit of insanity, in terror of not
succeeding;

on the contrary, he had just succeeded and had just discovered
what he was and who he was, when the collective conscience of society
punished him for tearing himself away from it, and
suicided him.

And it happened to Van Gogh as it usually happens, during an
orgy, a mass, an absolution or any other rite of consecration, posses-
sion, succubation or incubation.

So it introduced itself into his body,
this society
absolved
consecrated
sanctified
and possessed of the devil
effaced the supernatural consciousness that he had just acquired,
and like a flood of black crows in the fibers of his internal tree,
submerged him in a last swell
and, taking his place,
killed him.

For it is the anatomical logic of modern man to never have been able to live nor think of living except as one possessed.

### the man suicided by society

For a long time pure linear painting drove me mad until I met Van Gogh, who painted neither lines nor shapes but inert things in nature as if they were having convulsions.

And inert.

Under the terrible blow of that inert force that everyone hints at, and which never became so obscure as when the whole world and present-day life had meddled in its elucidation.

Now, it's with his club, really with a club, that Van Gogh never ceases battering at all forms of nature and objects.

Carded with Van Gogh's nail,

landscapes reveal their hostile flesh,

the snarl of their eviscerated meanderings,

so that no one knows, on the other hand, what strange force is in the process of being metamorphosed.

An exhibit of Van Gogh's paintings is always an historical event, not in the history of painted things but in plain historical history.

For there is no famine, no epidemic, no volcanic eruption, no earthquake, no war that heads off the monads of the air that wring the neck of the grim face of fama fatum and the neurotic destiny of things,

like a Van Gogh painting — brought out into the sunlight, and put directly back into view,

hearing, touch,

smell,

onto the walls of an exhibition hall —

finally launched anew into present actuality, reintroduced into circulation.

All the very great canvasses of the unhappy painter are not shown in the latest exhibit of Van Gogh at the Orangerie. But among those there, there are enough gyratory parades starred with tufts of carmine plants, of hollow lanes topped with yew trees, purplish suns spinning around over stacks of pure gold wheat, *Le Père Tranquille (The Old Benchwarmer)* and portraits of Van Gogh by Van Gogh,

to recall from what a sordid simplicity of objects, people, materials, elements,

Van Gogh has extracted those peculiar organ tones, those fire-works, those atmospheric epiphanies, in short, the 'great work' of a sempiternal tempestuous transmutation.

Those crows painted 2 days before he died did no more than any of his other paintings to open the door to a certain posthumous glory, but they revealed to painted painting or rather to unpainted nature, the secret door to a possible beyond, to a possible permanent reality, through the door opened by Van Gogh onto an enigmatic and sinister beyond.

It is no ordinary thing to see a man, who has the bullet that felled him lodged in his belly, stuffing a canvas with black crows and beneath them a plain, livid perhaps, but empty at any rate, where the winey color of the earth clashes wildly with the dirty yellow of the wheat.

But no other painter except Van Gogh would know how to find, the way he did, the truffle-black he used to paint the crows, that 'rich banquet' black and, at the same time, the excrement-like black of the crows' wings caught by the dwindling light of the evening.

And what is the earth below complaining about under the wings of the *splendid* crows? Splendor for Van Gogh alone, no doubt, and on the other hand the splendid augury of an evil that can no longer touch him?

The sky in the painting is low, brooding,

purplish like the shoulders of lightning.

The weird gloomy fringe of the void surging up after the flash.

Van Gogh released his crows, like the black microbes of his suicide's spleen, a few centimeters from the top and *the same at the bottom of his canvas,*

following the black gash of the line where the flapping of their rich feathers threatens with suffocation from on high the reswirling of an earthly storm.

And yet the whole picture is rich
the picture is rich, sumptuous and calm.

Worthy accompaniment to the death of the man who, during his lifetime, made so many drunken lines spin around so many unbound haystacks, and who in desperation, a bullet in his belly, could not help flooding a landscape with blood and wine, drenching the earth with a final emulsion, happy and gloomy at the same time, with a taste of sour wine and turned vinegar.

This is how the tone of the last picture painted by Van Gogh, never transcending painting, evoked the abrupt and barbaric quality of the most pathetic, impassioned and passionate Elizabethan drama.

It is what strikes me the most in Van Gogh, the painter of painters, who, without going any further in what is called painting, and what *is* painting, neither setting aside the tube, nor the brush, nor the framework, nor the *motif*, nor the canvas, nor the intrinsic beauty of the subject or the object, managed to impassion nature and objects to such a degree that the fabulous stories of Edgar Allen Poe, Herman Melville, Nathaniel Hawthorn, Gérard de Nerval, Achim Arnim or Hoffman say no more on the psychological and dramatic plane than these two-penny canvasses.

Most of his canvasses were of moderate dimensions as though he had chosen them that way on purpose.

A candlestick on a chair, on a green straw-bottomed armchair,
a book on the armchair,
and there the drama is revealed.
Who will enter?
Will it be Gauguin or some other ghost?

The lit candle on the armchair seems to indicate the line of luminous demarcation separating the 2 antagonistic individuals, Van Gogh and Gauguin.

The esthetic object of their quarrel would not, if related here, be of much interest perhaps, but it showed that there was a basic human schism between the personalities of Van Gogh and Gauguin.

I believe that Gauguin thought that an artist should seek the symbol, the myth, enlarge the things of life and raise them to the stature of the myth,

while Van Gogh believed that the myth should be deduced from the most earthy things in life.

And I think he was damned right.

Because reality is terribly superior to all history, to all fable, to all divinity, to all surreality.

All that is needed is the genius to interpret it,

which no painter before poor Van Gogh had done,

which no painter after him will,

for I believe that this time,

today,

now

in this month of February 1947,

it is reality itself,

the myth of reality itself, mythical reality itself which is materializing.

That is why no one since Van Gogh has known how to shake the great cymbal, the superhuman gong, perpetually superhuman, following the frustrated order from which real-life objects ring out,

when one has known how to open one's ears to understand the surging of their tidal-flow.

That is how the light of the candle rings forth, that the glow from the candlestick on the green straw-bottomed chair rings out like the breathing of a loving body near the body of a sleeping invalid.

It rings out like a strange criticism, a deep surprising judgement, and it seems that later, much later, the day when the violet light of the straw-bottomed chair will have submerged the picture, Van Gogh might allow us to guess at its sentence.

And it is impossible not to notice the patch of lavender light that devours the rungs of the great green armchair, the old armchair woven with green straw, even though one may not notice it immediately.

For it seems that the focal point is placed elsewhere, and its source appears to be strangely obscene, like a secret whose key Van Gogh must have kept on his person.

If Van Gogh had not died at the age of 37, I would not think of calling upon the Professional Mourner to announce with what supreme masterpieces painting might have been enriched,

because I cannot, after the 'Crows,' make myself believe that Van Gogh could have ever painted another canvas.

I think that he died at 37 because, alas, he had reached the end of the dismal and revolting story of a man garroted by an evil spirit.

For it is not because of himself nor the disease of his own insanity that Van Gogh quit life.

It was under the pressure of the evil spirit called Doctor Gachet, improvised psychiatrist, who, two days before his death, was the direct effectual and sufficient cause for his demise.

I have come to the firm and sincere conclusion, after reading Van Gogh's letters, that Dr. Gachet 'psychiatrist' really detested Van Gogh the painter, that he detested him not only as a painter but above all as a genius.

It is almost impossible to be a doctor and an honest man, but shamefully impossible to be a psychiatrist without bearing the stigma of the most indisputable insanity at the same time: this insanity cannot combat the old atavistic reflex of the black earth that makes every scientist caught in this black earth a kind of born innate enemy of all geniuses.

Medicine is born of evil, if it is not born of disease, and it has even, on the contrary, provoked sickness out of whole cloth in order to give itself a reason for being; but psychiatry is born of the vulgar black earth of people who have wished to maintain the evil at the source of illness and who have thus rooted out of their own nothingness a kind of Swiss Guard, to sap the rebellious drive which is the origin of all geniuses.

In every demented soul there is a misunderstood genius who frightens people and who has never found an escape from the stranglings that life has prepared for him, except in delirium.

Dr. Gachet never told Van Gogh that he was there to reform his painting (as Dr. Gaston Ferdière, head doctor at the Rodez Asylum, told me he was there to reform my poetry), but instead sent him out to paint from nature, to bury himself in a landscape to avoid the pain of thinking.

Only as soon as Van Gogh turned his head, Dr. Gachet would cut all contact with him.

As though not intending any harm, but simply by turning up his nose at a harmless trifle, by which gesture all the heedless bourgeois of the earth have registered the old magic force of a thought frustrated a hundred times.

In doing this, it was not only the evil of the problem that Dr. Gachet forbade him,

but the demoniacal seed,

the pangs of the screw turning in the gullet of the only passage,

with which Van Gogh,

tetanized,

hanging over the chasm of life,

painted.

For Van Gogh was terribly sensitive.

To be convinced of this just look at his seemingly panting face, which is also, from certain angles, the spellbinding face of a butcher.

That badly-lit face of an ancient butcher, sober-minded and finally retired from business, haunts me.

Van Gogh has portrayed himself in a considerable number of canvasses, and no matter how well-lit they may have been, I always have the painful impression that someone has falsified the meaning of the light that was needed to dig and map the way within him.

And it was certainly not Dr. Gachet who could show him the way.

But as I have said, in every living psychiatrist there exists a revolting and sordid atavism that makes him find an enemy in every artist, in every genius.

And I know that Dr. Gachet has left the impression in history, with regard to Van Gogh, whom he took care of, and who finally committed suicide while under his care, that he was the painter's last friend on earth, a sort of providential consoler.

Yet I believe more than ever that it was because of Dr. Gachet of Anvers-sur-Oise that Van Gogh had to, that day, the day he committed suicide at Anvers-sur-Oise,

had to, I repeat, quit life —

for Van Gogh was a creature of superior lucidity which enabled him, in any circumstances, to see further, infinitely and dangerously further than the immediate and apparent reality of facts.

What I mean to say about consciousness is that consciousness is in the habit of clinging to apparent reality.

In the depths of his naked butcher's eye Van Gogh committed himself without interruption to one of those melancholy alchemistic operations that took nature for object and the human body as a kettle or melting-pot.

And I know that Dr. Gachet always thought that it tired him.

Which was not, in his case, the result of simple medical concern, but the avowal of a jealousy as conscious as it was unacknowledged.

The reason for this was that Van Gogh had reached a stage of illumination in which disorderly thought surged back through the invading discharges of matter,

and where thinking is no longer exhausting,

*and no longer exists*

and where the only thing is *to gather bodies,* I mean

## TO PILE UP BODIES

It is no longer the astral world but one of direct creation which is understood beyond consciousness and the brain.

And I have never heard that a brainless body was ever fatigued by inert piers.

Piers of the inert, those bridges, those sun-flowers, those yews, those olive-gatherings, those haymakings. They no longer move.

They are frozen there.

But who could dream of their being harder under the razor's edge that unsealed their impenetrable quiver.

No, Dr. Gachet, a pier never tired anybody. These are the forces of a madman that give rest without causing motion.

I am also like poor Van Gogh, I no longer think, but every day I come closer to tremendous inner turmoils, and I would like to see some medical authority or other reproach me for tiring myself.

Someone owed Van Gogh a certain sum of money and, according to the story, Van Gogh had been fuming about it for several days.

The inclination of lofty natures, always a notch above reality, is to explain everything by a guilty conscience,

to believe that nothing is ever due to chance, and that everything bad that happens happens because of a conscious, intelligent concerted ill-will.

Which psychiatrists never believe.

Which geniuses always believe.

When I am sick it means that a spell has been cast upon me, and I cannot believe that I am sick, if I don't believe, on the other hand, that it is to someone's advantage to rob me of my health and profit by my health.

Van Gogh also thought that he was bewitched and said so.

And I, I know perfectly well that he was, and some day I will tell where and how.

And Dr. Gachet was that grotesque Cerberus, that slimy and purulent Cerberus, in sky-blue jacket and over-starched linen, who was placed in front of Van Gogh to strip him of all his sane ideas. For if his way of seeing, which was sane, were unanimously widespread, Society could no longer survive, but I know heroes of the earth who would find their freedom there.

Van Gogh could not shake off in time the kind of family vampirism that wanted Van Gogh the painter to stick to painting, but which, at the same time, denied him the right to claim the revolt necessary to the bodily and physical blossoming of his visionary personality.

There were any number of those stinking family confabulations between Theo and Dr. Gachet and the directors of insane asylums concerning the *patient* brought there.

147

' Make sure that he entertains no more of these ideas.' ' You see, the doctor says so, you must dismiss all those ideas. They're doing you harm. If you continue like that you'll be confined for the rest of your life.'

' You were promised that sum would be paid you. It will be paid. You cannot go on that way persisting in attributing the delay to ill-will.'

So there you have those good-natured psychiatrists' conversations which seem to be perfectly harmless, but they leave the trace of a small black tongue in the heart, the small black anodyne tongue of a poisonous salamander.

Sometimes that is all that is needed to lead a genius to suicide.

There are days when the soul feels the block so terribly that it is stricken, as if with a blow on the head, with the idea that it can no longer go on.

For it was precisely after one of these conversations with Dr. Gachet that Van Gogh went to his room, as if nothing had happened, and committed suicide.

I, myself, spent 9 years in an insane asylum and never had any suicidal tendencies, but I know that every conversation I had with a psychiatrist during the morning visit made me long to hang myself because I was aware that I could not slit his throat.

Theo was perhaps materially very good to his brother, but it did not prevent him from thinking him demented, a visionary with hallucinations, and furthermore he persisted in this way of thinking instead of going along with his brother's delirium,

to calm him.

What does it matter that he later died of sorrow?

The most important thing in the world to Van Gogh was his painter's imagination, his terrible, fanatical, apocalyptic visionary's imagination.

The world had to follow the order of its own womb, resume its compressed, anti-psychic rhythm of the occult public festival which, in front of everybody, had been put back into the white-hot melting-pot.

This means that the apocalypse, a completed apocalypse, is at this hour smouldering in Old Martyred Van Gogh's pictures, and that the world needs him in order to lash out with head and feet.

No one has ever written or painted, sculpted, modelled, built, invented, except to get out of hell.

And to get out of hell, I prefer the landscapes of this quiet convulsive man to the swarming compositions of Breughel the Elder or Hieronymus Bosch, who, compared to him, are only artists while Van Gogh is only a poor ignoramus determined not to deceive himself.

But, how can I make a scientist understand that there is something definitely insane in differential calculus, in the quantum theory, or in the obscene and absurd liturgical ordeals of the equinoctial precessions — because of that shrimp-colored eiderdown that Van Gogh froths up so gently in a chosen spot on his bed, because of the Veronese green, and the azure-drenched insurrection of that boat in front of which a washer-woman of Auvers-sur-Oise rises to her feet after work, because of that sun screwed behind the gray angle of the pointed village steeple over there, beyond that enormous mass of earth that seeks the wave where it can freeze in the foreground of magic colors.

O VIO PROFE

O VIO PROTO

O VIO LOTO

O THETHE

How senseless to describe a Van Gogh painting! No description attempted by anyone else can be compared to the simple alignment of natural objects and shades to which Van Gogh himself surrenders,

as great a writer as a painter, giving the impression of the most astounding authenticity in describing his work.


*July* 23rd 1890

' You will perhaps see the sketch of the gardener of Daubigny — it is one of my most deliberate pictures — I'm enclosing a sketch of old straw, and the sketches of two 18-inch canvasses depicting immense stretches of wheat after rain. . .

' Daubigny's garden with a foreground of green and pink grass.

149

To the left a green and lavender bush and the stump of a plant with whitish foliage. In the middle of a bed of roses, to the right, a hurdle, a wall, and above the wall a purple-leafed hazel-tree. Then a hedge of lilac, a row of rounded linden trees, the house itself in the background, pink with bluish tiles on the roof. A bench and three chairs, a black figure with a yellow hat, in the foreground a black cat. Pale green sky.'

### September 8th 1888

' In my painting *Night Café*, I have tried to show that the café is a place where one can come to ruin, go mad, commit crimes. I've tried with contrasts of tender pinks, blood red, and wine red, soft Louis XV and Veronese greens, contrasting with yellow greens and plain greens, hard whites, all together in the atmosphere of an infernal furnace of pale sulphur yellow, to express, so to speak, the power of the gloom of a dive.

' All this under a pretense of Japanese gaiety and the good-fellow-ship of *Tartarin*. . .

' What is drawing? How does one do it? It's the action for forcing one's way through an invisible iron wall which seems to be located somewhere between what one feels and what one can do. How does one get through this wall, for it is useless to hit it hard, it has to be undermined and penetrated with a file, slowly and with patience, as I see it.'

.........................................

It seems so easy to write like that.

Well! Go ahead and try. And tell me, since you are not the author of a Van Gogh picture, whether you could describe it so simply, so succinctly, objectively, durably, validly, solidly, opaquely, massively, authentically and miraculously as in this little letter of his.

(For the key criterion is not a question of degree nor cramp but the simple personal force of the fist.)

Therefore, I shall not describe one of Van Gogh's paintings after Van Gogh has done it, but I will say that Van Gogh is a painter because he re-collected nature as if he had re-perspired it and made it sweat, made it spurt forth in luminous beams onto his canvas, in monumental clusters of colors, the secular crushing of elements, the fearful elementary pressure of apostrophes, stripes, commas, bars, and we can no longer believe, after him, that the natural aspects of nature are not made up of these things.

And how many secret elbow-rubbings, ocular clashes taken from life, blinkings taken from nature, luminous currents of strength that prey on reality, have had to upset the barrier before finally being driven back and hoisted onto the canvas, as it were, and accepted.

There are no ghosts in Van Gogh's pictures, no visions, no hallucinations.

This is the torrid truth of a 2 p.m. sun.

A slow fertile nightmare elucidated little by little.

Without nightmare and without effect.

But pre-natal suffering is there.

It is the wet sheen of a pasture, of the flat surface of a wheat field which is there, ready to be uprooted.

And one day nature will have to take this into account.

Just as society will have to reckon with his premature death.

The flat surface of a wheat field bowed by the wind, and above it the wings of a single bird placed there like a comma. What painter who is not strictly speaking a painter, would have the audacity, like Van Gogh, to attack a subject of such disarming simplicity?

No, there are no ghosts in Van Gogh's pictures, no dramas, no subjects, and I might even say no objects, for what is the motif itself?

If not something akin to the iron shadow of the motet of some ineffable ancient music, like the leit-motif of a theme in despair over its own subject?

It is nature naked and pure, seen exactly as she reveals herself if tackled at close range.

Witness this landscape of melted gold, of bronze baked in Ancient Egypt, where an enormous sun leans heavily on rooftops so cowered under the light that they seem to be in a state of decomposition.

And I know of no apocalyptic, hieroglyphic, ghost-like or pathetic painting that gives me such a sensation of occult weirdness, of feeling like the corpse of useless occlusion, head split open, revealing its secret on the executioner's block.

As I say this I am not thinking of the Old Benchwarmer, nor of that fantastic autumn lane where a bent old man passes by with an umbrella caught on his sleeve like a rag-picker's hook.

I am recalling those crows with wings as black as lustrous truffles.

I am recalling his wheat field; ear upon ear of wheat and all is said, with, in front, a few poppies, gently scattered, pungently and nervously planted there, thinly sown, purposely and furiously punctuated and shredded.

Only life can offer the kind of epidermic stripping that speaks under an unbuttoned shirt, and no one knows why the eye leans to the left rather than to the right, toward the mound of curly hair.

But that's the way it is and it's a fact.

But that's the way it is and that's that.

His bedroom occult too, so adorably peasant-like and reeking of an odor that could conserve the wheat seen swaying in the landscape far away, through the window that would hide it.

Peasant-like too, the color of the old eiderdown, mussel-red, sea urchin-red, shrimp-red, mullet-of-the-Midi-red, scorched pimento-red.

And it is certainly Van Gogh's fault if the color of the eiderdown on his bed attained such reality, and I can think of no weaver who could transplant its ineffable stamp, as Van Gogh, from the depths of his mind, could convey the red of that ineffable glaze.

And I do not know how many criminal priests, dreaming in the head of their so-called Holy Ghost of the ochrous yellow and the infinite blue of a stained-glass window to their harlot ' Mary,' could isolate in the air, extract from the cunning niches of the air, such simple colors which are an event in themselves, and where each stroke of Van Gogh's brush on the canvas is much more than an event.

Sometimes it looks like a tidy room, but with a coating of balm or an aroma that no Benedictine monk could find to give the finishing touch to his healthy liqueurs.

152

(That room recalls the end-product, with its pearl-white wall on which hangs a rough towel like an old peasant charm, unapproachable but comforting.)

Another time it gives the effect of a simple haystack crushed by an enormous sun.

There are those light chalk-whites that are worse than ancient tortures, and more than ever in that painting does poor Van Gogh's scrupulous honesty appear.

For Van Gogh will prove to have been the real painter of painters, heavily and pathetically applied. The common color of things, but oh so right, so lovingly right that there are no precious stones that can equal its rarity.

For Van Gogh is all that, the unique scrupulousness of the stroke the only one who had no wish to go beyond painting; he stuck to the strict means of his trade and the strict framework of his means.

And on the other hand the only one, absolutely the only one, who absolutely went beyond painting, the inert act of representing nature, in order to create a revolving force, an element plucked straight from the heart.

With his way of representing things he soldered air and enclosed a nerve in it, which does not exist in nature, but a truer air or nerve than his cannot be found in nature.

As I write these lines, I see the bloody red face of the painter coming at me, from a wall of eviscerated sunflowers,

from a tremendous embrasure of opaque hyacinths and fields of lapis-lazuli.

All of it, amid a meteoric bombardment of atoms falling grain by grain,

proof that Van Gogh thought of his canvasses as a painter would, indeed, and only as a painter, but who would be

by *that very fact*

a tremendous musician.

Organist of an arrested tempest that laughs in limpid nature, pacified between two torments; but this nature, like Van Gogh himself, shows that he is quite ready to kick the dust from his feet.

After having seen him it is quite possible to turn away from any other painted canvas, for it has nothing more to tell us. The stormy light of Van Gogh's painting begins its somber recitations at the very moment we have ceased looking at it.

Nothing but a painter, Van Gogh, and nothing more, no philosophy, no mysticism, no rite, no *physcurgy*, no liturgy,

no history, literature or poetry, those bronze-gold sunflowers are painted: they are painted like sunflowers and nothing more, but to understand a sunflower in nature, it's necessary now to go back to Van Gogh; just as to understand a storm in nature,

a stormy sky,

a plain in nature,

it will be forever impossible not to refer to Van Gogh.


It was stormy like that in Egypt or on the plains of Semitic Judaea,

perhaps it was dark like that in Chaldea, in Mongolia, or on the Mountains of Tibet, and no one has ever told me that they have been moved.

And yet, looking at that field of wheat or rocks as bleached as a heap of buried bones, over which that purplish sky broods, I can no longer believe in the Mountains of Tibet.

As a painter, and nothing else but a painter, Van Gogh adopted the methods of pure painting and never went beyond them.

I mean that in order to paint he used no other methods than those that painting afforded him.

A stormy sky,

a chalk-white plain,

canvasses, brushes, his own red hair, tubes, his yellow hand, his easel,

but all the lamas in Tibet can shake, under their robes, the apocalypse they will have prepared;

Van Gogh will have given us an inkling of the nitrogen peroxide in a canvas that depicts just enough sinister things to force us to get our bearings.

One fine day he decided not to surpass the motif,

but when Van Gogh's work has been seen, one can no longer believe that there is anything less surpassable than the motif.

The simple motif of a lighted candle on a straw armchair, with a purplish frame, tells a great deal more under Van Gogh's brush than the whole series of Greek tragedies, or the plays of Cyril Turner, Webster, or Ford, which, incidentally, have never been played.

Without being literary, I have seen Van Gogh's face, red with blood in the explosions of his landscapes, coming at me

   KOHAN
   TAVER
   TINSUR
   And yet,

in a burning,

in a bombardment,

in an explosion,

avengers of that millstone that Van Gogh the madman wore around his neck all his life.

The torture of painting without knowing why or where.


For it is not for this world that we have always worked,

struggled,

brayed against the horrors of hunger, misery, hatred, scandal, disgust

that we were all poisoned,

even though we were all enthralled by these things,

and because of which we finally committed suicide;

for are we not all like poor Van Gogh, men suicided by society!


Van Gogh refused to tell stories in his paintings, but the marvelous thing is that this painter was only a painter,

and more of a painter than other painters, as if he were a man for whom the material, and painting itself, held a place of prime importance, with color seized as if just pressed out of the tube,

with the imprint of each hair of his brush in the color,

with the texture of the painted paint, distinct in its own sunlight,

with the I, the comma, the period of the point of the brush itself screwed right onto the hearty color that spurts forth in forks of fire which the painter tames and remixes everywhere,

the marvelous thing is, this painter who was nothing more than a painter but also, among all the existing painters, is the one who makes us forget that we are dealing with painting,

with painting to represent the subject he has distinguished,

evoking for us, in front of the fixed canvas, the enigma pure, the pure enigma of a tortured flower, of a landscape slashed, pressed and plowed on all sides by his drunken brush.

His landscapes are old sins that have not yet found their primitive apocalypses, but will not fail to do so.

Why do Van Gogh's paintings give me the impression of being seen from the other side of the tomb, from a world where finally his suns will have been the only things that spun around and lit up joyously?

For is it not the whole history of what was one day called the soul which lives and dies in his convulsive landscapes and flowers?

The soul that gave its ear to the body, and that Van Gogh returned to the soul of his soul,

a woman, to give body to the sinister illusion —

one day the soul did not exist,

nor the mind,

as for consciousness, no one had ever thought of it,

and, besides, where was thought in a world made up entirely of warring elements recomposed as soon as they were destroyed,

for thought is a luxury of peace,

and who is better than the incredible Van Gogh, the painter who understood the phenomenal side of the problem, he for whom any real landscape was in a way controlled in the melting-pot where it would be brewed all over again?

So old Van Gogh was King, against whom while he was sleeping, the strange sin called Turkish culture was invented,

example, habitat, the motive for the sin of humanity, which never knew anything else but to devour artists in the raw in order to reinforce its own honesty.

Wherein it has only ritually consecrated its cowardice!

For mankind does not want to take the trouble to live, to take part in the spiritual elbowing of the forces that make up reality, in order to pluck a body from them so that no tempest could ever again harm it.

It has always preferred mere existence.

As for life, it seeks the artist within his own genius.

Therefore Van Gogh, who cooked one of his own hands, was never afraid of a struggle in order to live, that is to say, to disassociate the reality of living from the idea of existing,

and naturally, everything can exist without taking the trouble to be,

unlike Van Gogh the madman, everything can exist without taking the trouble to radiate and glow.

That is what society took away from Van Gogh in order to carry out its Turkish culture, which has a facade of honesty and which is in itself the prop and the origin of crime.

That is why Van Gogh died suicided, because it was the concerted awareness of society as a whole that could bear him no longer.

For if there was neither spirit, nor soul, nor conscience, nor thought,

there was the fulminate

of a ripe volcano,

of trance-stone,

of patience,

of tumors,

of cooked tumors,

and of the bed-sores of a skinned man.

And King Van Gogh dozed, hatching the next alert for the coming insurrection of his health.

How?

By the fact that good health is a plethora of deep-seated ills, of a tremendous zest for living, through a thousand corroded wounds, which must be forced to live,

which must be induced to perpetuate themselves.

He who does not smell of a smouldering bomb and of compressed vertigo is not worthy to be alive.

This is the solace that poor Van Gogh took upon himself to reveal in a burst of flame.

But the evil that watched over him wounded him.

The Turk, with his honest face, approached Van Gogh delicately, to pluck the sugared almond from within him,

in order to detach the (natural) sugared almond that was forming.

And Van Gogh wasted a thousand summers there.

He died of this at 37,

before living,

for every monkey had lived before him with forces that he had assembled.

And that is what must now be restored in order to bring Van Gogh back to life.

Compared to a humanity of cowardly monkeys and wet dogs, Van Gogh's painting will prove to have belonged to a time when there was no soul, no mind, no consciousness, no thought, only raw elements alternately enchained and unchained.

Landscapes of strong convulsions, of insane traumas, as of a body that fever torments in order to restore it to perfect health.

Under the skin the body is an over-heated factory,

and outside,

the invalid shines,

glows,

from every burst pore;

such is a Van Gogh

landscape

at noon.

Only perpetual struggle explains a peace that is only transitory,

just as milk that is ready to be poured explains the kettle in which it has boiled.

One day Van Gogh's painting, armed with fever and good health, will return to toss the dust of a caged world into the air, a world Beware of Van Gogh's beautiful landscapes whirling and peaceful. that his heart could no longer bear.

*p o s t - s c r i p t u m*

To come back to the painting of the crows.

Who has ever seen, as in this canvas, land equal to the sea?

Van Gogh, of all painters, is the one who strips us down the furthest, and right down to the thread, just as one would delouse oneself of an obsession.

Of making objects look different, finally of risking the sin of the *alter-ego,* and the earth cannot take on the color of a liquid sea, and yet, with his hoe Van Gogh tosses his earth like a liquid sea.

And he infused his canvas with the color of the dregs of wine, and it is the earth that smells of wine, still splashing among the waves of wheat, rearing a somber cockscomb against the low clouds gathering in the sky on all sides.

But, as I have already said, the funereal part of the story is the opulence with which the crows are treated.

That color of musk, of rich nard, of truffles from a great banquet.

In the purplish waves of the sky, two or three heads of old men made of smoke venture an apocalyptic grimace, but Van Gogh's crows are there inciting them to be more decent, I mean inciting them to less spirituality,

that is what Van Gogh meant in this canvas with its underslung sky, painted at almost the exact moment that he was delivering himself of life, for on the other hand this work has the strange almost pompous aspect of birth, marriage, departure.

I hear the wings of the crows beating cymbals loudly above a world whose flood Van Gogh can apparently no longer contain.

Then, death.

The olive trees of Saint Rémy.

The solitary cypress.

159

The bedroom.

The promenades.

The Arles Café.

The bridge where one feels like plunging one's finger in the water, in a gesture of violent regression to a state of childhood forced upon one by Van Gogh's amazing grip.

The water is blue,

not a water-blue,

but a liquid paint blue.

The suicided madman has been there and given the water of paint back to nature,

but who will give it back to him?

Van Gogh, a madman?

let him who once knew how to look at a human face take a look at the self-portrait of Van Gogh, I am thinking of the one with the soft hat.

Painted by an extra-lucid Van Gogh, that face of a red-headed butcher, inspecting and watching us, scrutinizing us with a glowering eye.

I do not know of a single psychiatrist who would know how to scrutinize a man's face with such overpowering strength, dissecting its irrefutable psychology as if with a knife.

Van Gogh's eye belongs to a great genius, but from the way I see him dissecting me, surging forth from the depths of the canvas, it is no longer the genius of a painter that I feel living within him at this moment, but the genius of a certain philosopher never encountered by me in this life.

No, Socrates did not have this eye; perhaps the only one before Van Gogh was the unhappy Nietzsche who had the same power to undress the soul, to pluck the body from the soul, to lay the body of man bare, beyond the subterfuges of the mind.

Van Gogh's gaze is hanging, screwed, glazed behind his naked eyelids, his thin wrinkleless eyebrows.

It is a look that penetrates, pierces, in a face roughly-hewn like a well-squared tree.

But Van Gogh chose the moment when the pupil of the eye is going to spill into emptiness,

where this glance, aimed at us like the bomb of a meteor, takes on the atonal color of the void and inertia that fills it.

This is how Van Gogh located his illness, better than any psychiatrist in the world.

I pierce, I resume, I inspect, I cling to, I unseal, my dead life conceals nothing, and, after all, nothingness has never harmed anyone. What forces me to withdraw within myself is that disheartening absence that passes and overwhelms me at times, but I perceive it clearly, very clearly, I even know what nothingness is, and could even say what is inside it.

And Van Gogh was right, one can live for the infinite, and only be satisfied with infinite things, there is enough of the infinite on the earth and in the spheres to satisfy a thousand great geniuses, and if Van Gogh was unable to satisfy the desire to fill his life with it, it is simply that society forbade it.

Flatly and consciously forbade it.

One day Van Gogh's executioners arrived, as they did for Gérard de Nerval, Baudelaire, Edgar Allen Poe and Lautréamont.

Those who one day said to him:

And now, enough, Van Gogh, to your grave, we've had our fill of your genius, and as for the infinite, the infinite belongs to us.

For it is not because of his search for the infinite that Van Gogh died,

obliged to choke with misery and asphyxiation,

he died from seeing the infinite refused him by the rabble of all those who thought to withhold it from him during his own life;

and Van Gogh could have found enough infinite to live on for his whole life-span had not the bestial mind of the masses wanted to appropriate it to feed their own debaucheries, which have never had anything to do with painting or poetry.

Besides, one does not commit suicide alone.

No one was ever born alone.

Nor has anyone died alone.

But, in the case of suicide, a whole army of evil beings is needed to force the body to perform the unnatural act of depriving itself of its own life.

And I believe that there is always someone else, at the extreme moment of death, to strip us of our own life.

And thus, Van Gogh condemned himself because he had finished with living, and we gather this from his letters to his brother; because of the birth of his brother's son,

he felt that he himself would be one mouth too many to feed.

But above all Van Gogh wanted to join that infinite for which, said he, one embarks as on a train to a star,

and one embarks the day one has finally decided to finish with life.

Now in Van Gogh's death, as it actually occurred, I do not believe that is what happened.

Van Gogh was dispatched from this earth by his brother, first by announcing the birth of his nephew, and he was sent away by Dr. Gachet who, instead of recommending rest and solitude, sent him off to paint from nature, a day when he was well aware that it would have been better for Van Gogh to go to bed.

For lucidity and sensibility such as the martyred Van Gogh possessed cannot be so obviously thwarted.

There are souls who, on certain days, would kill themselves over a simple contradiction, and it isn't necessary to be insane for that, a registered and catalogued lunatic; on the contrary, it is enough to be in good health and to have reason on one's side.

I, in a similar situation, could no longer bear to hear, without committing a crime: 'Monsieur Artaud, you're raving,' as so often has happened to me.

And Van Gogh heard just that.

And that is what caused the knot of blood that killed him to twist in his throat.

## Post-scriptum

Concerning Van Gogh, magic and spells, all the people who have paraded before the exhibition of his works at the Orangerie for the last two months, are they really sure to remember all they did and everything that happened to them every night of the months of February, March, April and May 1946? Could there not have been one particular night when the atmosphere and the streets became liquid, gelatinous, unstable, and when the light of the stars and the celestial vault disappeared?

And Van Gogh was not there, he who painted the Arles Café. But I was at Rodez, that is to say, still on earth, while all the inhabitants of Paris must have felt, all one night, very close to leaving it.

And was this not because they had participated in unison in certain generalized dirty tricks, when the consciousness of Parisians left its normal level for an hour or two and proceeded to another one, one of those mass unfurlings of hatred which I have witnessed so many times during my nine years of internment.

Now hatred is forgotten like the nocturnal expurgations that follow, and the same ones who so many times bared their swinish souls to the whole world now file past Van Gogh, whose neck they or their fathers and mothers so well wrung when he was alive.

But was it not one of those evenings I have been talking about that an enormous white stone fell on the Boulevard de la Madeleine at the corner of the Rue des Mathurins, as if shot from a recent volcanic eruption of the volcano Popocatepetl?

*Translated by Mary Beach*
*+ Lawrence Ferlinghetti*

# LETTER TO PIERRE LOEB

The time man was a tree without organs or function
but only will
and was a tree walking at will
will return.
It was, and will return.
For the biggest lie ever was to frame man as an organism
of eating, assimilating,
incubating, excreting,
that which existed creating a whole hierarchy of latent functions
to elude the field of the *deliberate*

                              will,

the will which decides for itself at every moment;
for it's that that makes this human tree walk,
a will which decides for itself at every moment,
without occult subliminal functions controlled by an unconscious
out of what we are or wish to be, we are left very little in fact,
a bit of dust floating on the surface,
but what is the rest, Pierre Loeb?
An organism to ingurgitate,
to put on meat,
to excrete,
and in its sensory field,
like an iridescence,
far off,
a rainbow covenant with god
surviving,
floating,
the lost atoms,
the ideas,
accidents and chance happenings in the whole of a whole body.
What was Baudelaire,
what were Edgar Poe, Nietzsche, Gérard de Nerval?
BODIES they were

that ate,
digested,
slept,
snored once a night,
*shit*
between 25 and 30,000 times
in the face of 30 or 40,000 meals,
40 thousand sleeps,
40 thousand snores,
40 thousand mouths safe and sour on waking
each putting 50 poems out of himself,
not very much, really,
and the balance between *magical* and *automatic*
production is very far from being maintained,
in fact is absolutely ruined,
but *human* reality, Pierre Loeb, is not that.
We are 50 poems,
the rest is not us but the nothingness we are clothed in,
which first laughs at us,
then lives on us.
So this nothingness is nothing,
it isn't something,
it is some.
*I mean* some men.
Beasts with no will or thoughts of their own,
that is, no pain of their own,
no acceptance of the will of their own pain,
who never found any other way to live
except by counterfeiting being human.
And from the bodily tree of
pure will that we were,
they made this alembic of pure shit,
this barrel of fecal distillation
carrying pestilence
and all other diseases,

this aspect of hybrid feebleness,
this congenital flaw
which typifies THE BORN MAN.
One day man was virulent,
He was all electric nerve,
flames of an everlasting phosphorescence,
but that passed into fable
because the beasts got born,
the beasts,
these discrepencies of innate magnetism,
these empty gaps between breaths of power
*which never were,*
were nothingness
that became something,
and man's magical life was overthrown,
man fell from his magnetic rock
and the inspiration that was his true basis
became chance, accident,
rarity,
*excellence,*
excellence perhaps,
but in the face of such swarming horrors
he would have done better never to have been born.
It was no garden of eden,
it was a labor state,
proletarian,
the work
         without sloppiness, without waste.
Why wasn't this state maintained?
For reasons by which
the bestial organism, made of, for and by the beasts
which *for centuries* have usurped his rightful place,
*will explode.*
Exactly for the same reasons.
These reasons more inevitable than those.

And this explosion of the beast organism more inevitable
than that of the unique labor
in the effort of the unique and most undiscoverable will.
For actually the human tree,
human without functions or organs to justify being human,
this human went on being,
clothed in the other's fake, in
the other's fake clothing
he kept on being in his own will,
but hidden
and without compromise or contact with the other.
And that which was fallen was that which planned to surround and
imitate, and before long
in a blow like a bomb
will reveal
the other's inanity.
For a screen had to arise between the first human tree
and the others,
but for the others it needed time, centuries of time in order
that the men who have begun to achieve their body
like that which has never begun and never ceased achieving its
body
except by nothingness
and there is no body there
and *in the beginning there is nothing*

> And then?
> Then.

Then discrepencies were born between men and the dry work
of jamming nothingness.
Soon this work will be done.
The carapace has to give.
The carapace of this world.
Built on the digestive mutilations of a body that ten thousand
wars, and evil
and disease,

and misery,
and penury of goods, objects and substances of prime necessity
have ripped apart.
The upholders of the profit hierarchy,
of social and bourgeoise institutions
who never worked
but *accumulated* for thousands of years, bit by bit, the
stolen goods,
and keep them holed up in certain caves of powers
*defended by all humanity,*
with a small number of exceptions
will be forced to deploy their energy
and therefore fight
and they will be incapable of not fighting
for it's their eternal *cremation* which is coming at the end of the
war, this apocalyptic war coming on.
This is why I believe the conflict between America and
Russia,
even if it had twice the number of bombs,
is nothing much beside this other conflict,
which will

in one flash
*fuse*

the upholders of a digestive humanity
on the one side,
with this man
of pure will and his very rare adepts and followers on the other,
but who have the power of the

sempiternal
on their side.

*Translated by David Rattray*

# THEATRE AND SCIENCE

True theatre has always seemed to me the exercise of a
dangerous and terrible act
    where the idea of theatre and spectacle is done away with
    as well as the idea of all science, all religion and all art.
The act I'm talking about aims for a true organic and physical
transformation of the human body.
    Why?
Because theatre is not that scenic parade where one develops
virtually and symbolically — a myth: theatre is rather
    this crucible of fire and real meat where
    by an anatomical trampling of bone, limbs and syllables
          bodies are renewed
               and the mythical act of making a body presents itself
physically and plainly.

If you understand me correctly, you'll see in this an act
of true genesis that will seem to everybody much too absurd —
too silly, in fact — to perform
on the plane of real life.
    For as of now nobody believes a body can change except
through time and in death.
    Now, I repeat, death is an invented state
    and it keeps itself alive only through all the low rabble of
    warlocks, gurus and conjurers of
nothingness for whom it is profitable and who for some centuries now
have been nourished by it
          and live by it in the state called Bardo.
    Aside from that, the human body is immortal.
    It's that old story and must be brought up-to-date again by
head-on attack.
    The human body dies only because we have forgotten how to
transform it and change it.
    Beyond that it does not die, it does not fall into dust, it
does not pass through the tomb.

One of the vicious pleasantries of nothingness which religion,
society and science have thus obtained from human consciousness
is that of
inducing it at a given moment to leave its body,
of making it believe that the human body was
perishable and destined after a little while to ' bid adieu.'
No, the human body is imperishable and immortal and it changes,
it changes physically and materially
anatomically and manifestly,
it changes visibly and on the spot, provided
you are really willing to take the material trouble to make it change.
There once existed an operation of an order less magical than
scientific —
and which the theatre has only touched upon —
by which the human body,
when it was recognized as evil, was passed,
transported
physically and materially,
objectively, and as if molecularly, from one
body to another,
from a long gone and lost state of body
to a strengthened, risen state of body.
And for that it was enough to address yourself to all the dramatic,
driven-under and fugitive forces of the human body.
So the question here is revolution,
and everyone is crying out for a necessary revolution,
but I don't know if enough people have understood that this
revolution would not be real as long as it was not physically
and materially complete,
as long as it would not turn and face man,
face the body of man himself
and decide once and for all to demand that *he change*.
Now the body has become indecent and evil because we live in an
indecent and evil world which doesn't want the human body changed,
and which at its own disposition —

from all sides
and in every necessary direction —
has sent its occult and shadowy crew of galley-slaves
out everywhere to prevent this body from ever changing.

In this way the world is evil not only on the outside surface,
but subterraneously and secretly it cultivates and maintains the
evil which has made it so, and we have made it so that
everything is born from evil spirit and at the center of
evil spirit.

Not only morals are rotten, the very atmosphere
we live in is materially and physically rotten with actual poetry,
with obscene appearances, with venomous spirits, with infected
organisms which you can see with the naked eye provided you have,
like myself, lengthily, bitterly and systematically suffered from it.

And hallucinations or delirium are all out of the question here:
no, here
it is a question of this confirmed sophisticated elbow-pushing from
an abominable world of souls in which every imperishable actor, every
uncreated poet of the breath has always been made to feel the
shameful parties making filth of his purest flights.

And no political or moral revolution will be possible
so long as man continues to be magnetically held down —
even in his most elementary and simple organic and nervous
reactions —
by the sordid influence
of all the questionable centers of the Initiates,
who, sitting tight in the warmth of the electric blankets of their
duality-schism
laugh at revolutions as well as wars,
certain that the anatomical order on which the
existence as well as the duration of actual society is based
will no longer know how to be changed.

Now there are in the human breath sudden shifts and breaks of
tone and, from one scream to another, abrupt transferences
by which the openings and soarings of the entire body of things

can be suddenly evoked, which can support or liquify an organ like
a tree you might prop up against the massy mountain of its forest.

   Now

  the body has a breath and a scream by which it can act on the
decomposed lowest depths of the organism and visibly transport itself
up to those high brilliantly lighted planes where the Superior Body
is already waiting for it.

   In this operation, in the blindest depths of the organic
scream of catapulted breath, there

       pass all the possible states of blood and mood,

         the whole battle of splinters and prickles of the body
made visible,

  emerging from among the false monsters of the schism

   of spirituality

     and sensibility.

There have been incontestable periods in the history of time
when this physiological operation took place and where the evil
human Will never had the opportunity to gather its forces together
and evolve, as of now, its monsters issued from copulation.

If at certain points and for certain races, human sexuality
has arrived at this black spot,

  and if this sexuality breeds infected influences,

    hideous bodily poisons

      which at present are paralyzing

all effort of Will and sensibility

       and make impossible all attempts

at metamorphosis

     and a revolution that is definitive

      and

         complete —

  if so, it is because centuries have passed already

   which have refused a certain operation of the physiological
transmutation

    and true organic metamorphosis of the human body,

   and by their atrocity,

their material bugger ferocity
and their breadth
they have cast down into shadows of a lukewarm psychic night
all the psychological, logical or dialectical dramas of
the human heart.
I mean the body is keeping its breaths in irons,
and this breath binds the bodies whose throbbing
pressure
and hideous atmospheric compression sterilize,
whenever they arise,
all the impassioned or psychic states that consciousness
can evoke.
There is a degree of tension, of crush, of opaque density,
of the accumulated forcing-back of body
which leaves far behind all philosophy, all dialectic,
all music, all physics,
all poetry,
all magic.
I won't show you tonight what requires many hours
of progressive exercises to even begin to make itself visible;
besides I would need space and air,
and especially a head of steam I haven't got.
But you will certainly understand in the texts which
will be spoken
coming from those who speak them,
the screams
the unchained soarings of a sincerity which is on its way
to this revolution of the whole body without which nothing can
be changed.

*Translated by Daniel Moore*

# FRAGMENTATIONS

Out of the motherless cunt I shall make an obscure, total, obtuse and absolute soul.

●

Yesterday evening March 13th a party for Yvonne.
Children of animated stick people.
The etruscan terra cotta.

●

Being is that parasitism of the brain I made *dawn* in order to rid myself of god and his ministers: diseases, night.

●

It was born gradually, this indifference I have acquired like the most hardened tough before the coffin of my six daughters of the heart yet to be born:

> Yvonne,
> Catherine,
> Neneka,
> Cecile,
> Anna
> and
> Little Annie

●

Before they got away from me I had already trounced them into a shape worse than that god they came to only later.

●

Bigger on this floor where rigormortis was setting into the biggest one, not like a knee barbed with a kneecap, but like the infinitely small that advances into the angle of its sempiternal strangulation.

●

Which indeed is not in philosophy, but in the pot of fried potatoes, square perhaps, and with the scythe-handle handling like a spoon in the perforated tongue of the genital forever denied by the heart.

●

A dead little girl said: I'm the one who puffs horror into the legs of the live little girl. Get me out of here fast.

●

They breathed terms of dead wax on the reproved bodies of beings, and made stupefying retentions of them, who didn't exist before their birth but

insulin by insulin,

imagined they existed,

and yet the artichoke quivers on the handle when it is a virgin who makes caca.

Insulin is Ka without shit, shit without making caca.

●

There are only dead men

asleep in me;

some are free, they are on the outside;

the others are in this dungheap-hell where my shinbone keeps going out grazing, in order to excavate hell.

●

Yesterday evening March 15th the installation of my suffering, the dialectic entering me like the derision of my living flesh, which suffers and doesn't understand.

●

Morphine on a wooden leg. Done. This morphine with the gangrene of the bone of the dead leg. Then drawn off. That is what the

holy trinity was.

●

If we are to explain consciousness, it isn't enough to shake up the fluids, consciousness not being an *esprit de corps* but the volume of a body up to the point where it elbows its way into *existence,* against the mind that will suppurate it.

●

Sick minds are not mental states but beings who never were willing to

in-dure themselves.

●

The spirits will not bother with my affairs, and I will fix them forever with my hands and without a concept, like a workingman adjusting the parts of the body whose law is my sperm-box, and in the coffins of firingsquad stakes that my legs are.

●

But once a stake has gotten loose, it is no longer a question of adjusting the parts, but of making the stake explode into an irreplaceable member.

●

For the children of the principal *mise en scéne*
are not in the grunt but in the cunt,
which isn't the original garret of a law but a frightful chewing.
Not in the tone but in the cunt, extreme elbow of this bottom-blade which advances with its horrible denture of beings, created to swallow up all beings, who never know where they are.

●

In slumber you sleep: there is no self, nobody but ghosts,
the ghouls that snatch the *tetema* of being from that which makes us a body (they are other beings waking up at this moment).
And what is the *tetema*?
It's the blood of the body stretched out at that moment, dozing because it is sleeping. How can the *tetema* be blood? By the *ema*, before which reposes the *tee* and signifies that which reposes like the *teevee* of the people of Marseilles. For the *tee* makes a sound like a cinder when the tongue inserts it in the lips, where it will smoke.
And *Ema* in Greek means blood. And *tetema* means twice the cinder on the flame of the bloodclot, that inveterate bloodclot which is the body of the dreaming sleeper who would do better if he got up.
— For neither the unconscious nor the subconscious is the law.
Every dream is a piece of suffering torn out of us by other beings, by chance, with the monkey paw they throw upon me every night, the cinder in repose in our self, which isn't a cinder but a machine-gunning as if the blood were scrapiron and the self the ferruginous one.
And what is the ferruginous one?

176

It's this simplex: a head, a trunk on two legs, and two arms to jostle the trunk around in the sense of always continuing with a head, two arms and two legs.

For it has been said from time immemorial that the illiterate is a mystery, without alpha and omega but with a head, two arms and two legs. The hopeless illiterate of the simplex which is man and doesn't understand. He understands that he is head and arms, legs to get the trunk moving. And that there is nothing else but this: this totempole of ears eyelids and a nose perforated by twenty fingers.

And that is the mystery of man which god the mind has never stopped pestering.

•

There are no insides, no mind, no outsides or consciousness, nothing but the body as it may be seen — a body that doesn't stop existing, even when the eye that sees it falls.

And this body is a fact.

Myself.

•

Sperm is not a urination but a being who forever advances toward a being, to scorch it with itself.

•

This sperm is no fiction, but a war with thorn-crowned machine-gun barrels whose magazines churn themselves to a cream, like egg-beaters, before they *churn* into the breach of some ONE.

•

Operation whereby the fall of man took place, on the day he consented to play cunt.

•

And 2nd
secondly,
it wasn't nails but nothingness
which one day proclaimed itself a nail,
because it had rasped against my head too long and because I, Antonin Artaud, in order to punish it for sucking my head, turned it into a nail with one hammerblow.

177

I saw Yvonne's swollen sac, I saw the sac puffed up with the dregs of Yvonne's blistered soul, I saw that hideous soft sac of Yvonne's buggered soul, I saw Yvonne's ballooning heart punctured like an enormous swollen sac of pus, I saw the corpse of this dishonored Ophelia drifting not on the Milky Way but on the Way of human filthiness, in curses, agony, abomination, I saw the corpse of her who loved me exposed to the rancid belches of the soul slapped down and kicked,

I saw at last the swelling, the hideous dilation of this heart plagued for having tried to bring me a metalloid when I had nothing else to eat,

I saw this brown sac pass like the pus of despair, I saw my daughter's dead goiter, which life had seized upon to sprout and infect her, passing by.

I saw her sprout also, deathly bitter at having been dishonored.

•

I saw the corpse of my daughter Annie incinerated, and her sexual organs squandered and divided after her death by the police of France.

•

Priests are assholes without ego who are constantly talking into other people's assholes in order to plant their ego there.

•

I saw the meningeal syphilis of my daughter Catherine's legs, and the 2 hideous sweet-potatoes of the vats of her inflated kneecaps, I saw the onions of her toes blistered like her sex, which she has not been able to wash since last year when she began her trek here, I saw a skullburst like Annie of the 'holy' throat, and I saw her blood's crown of intestinal thorns flowing from her on the days she wasn't menstruating.

•

And I saw the nicked knife of Neneka, my other daughter, and I felt her moving in the opium of the earth,

and there were also Yvonne, Catherine, Cecile, Annie and Anna with Neneka.

And she was dental opium, for nothing is worse than a toothache.

The opium of the earth's canine teeth which everyone has been grinding underfoot.

She loved me one day when I was chewing in order to compose the earth, the earth which I will eat.

And I saw the human phallus beating the heart of Cecile with her teats,

in that slot of a bone-rack

where the catechistic soul smells death,

the open mouth of an imperishable cellar.

For the sacrificed blood smells of cinders in the casks of its cellar.

And how many testicles of hatred have flogged this firstborn heart?

There still remain Anna and Annie.

•

Infinity is pure chance, not god, and what is chance?

It's *myself*, I was told by myself, who listens to me.

And I answered myself: All my selves are there because, as far as I am concerned, I am not listening to you.

•

It was Anna who loved the music one day from the top of that shed that is listening to me when I am thinking, not of myself but of her. Who is her?

The soul that will be born from me.

That's all very fine, but when will I see Anna Corbin, on whose belly all the medicine passed, Anna Corbin known as the whore by all the *petitebourgeoises* tarts from St. Roch to Notre-Dame des Champs?

Anna Corbin, firstborn daughter of my soul, who died despairing of me.

Never!

Yes, one day, one day soon, when I'll finally be able to eat.

•

And to marry me, Anna Corbin shall have waited for the earth to be cleansed, like Yvonne, Cecile, Annie, Catherine, Neneka — those dead girls who, beyond the distress of their limbs, are waiting, before they come to me, until I have got done marrying my Ka Ka.

•

You have to eat earth, just once.

•

And I saw Martha Robert of Paris, I saw her from Rodez to Paris bent over with anger in the corner of my sealed room, just in front of the nighttable, like a flower extirpated with anger, in the apocalypse of life.

•

And there is also Colette Thomas to blow the gendarmes of hatred from Paris to Nagasaki.

She will explain to you her own tragedy.

P.S.

I had a dream last night, a jumbled dream, yes, by god, for a jumbled dream it really was jumbled; but on the other hand it was meaningful, extremely meaningful.

Jean Dequeker was dragging along on the ground with his legs lopped short, and he said: Am I a beast, a stone, a branch, or a stall?

But after all what is a tree? What is a tree?

Madame Dequeker was inside a cage, with her stomach pressed against the grillwork of the cage, saying: Is it that my own stomach, no . . .

(hey, aren't you my stomach?)

isn't it that my own stomach is going to finish up by rumbling?

Colette Thomas was a form full of Greek fire, and she bawled: If that doesn't stop, I blow.

Madame Dequeker, the aging lady, became invisible, like the tinfoil of a puddle of being that couldn't succeed in coming back, with her right hand in the air like an old membrane floating above the abdomen, and saying: I certainly would like my 2 hands joined without joints, but no joined hands, no, no joined hands. — But how difficult that is, how difficult. . .

*Translated by David Rattray*

# THE TALE OF POPOCATEPEL

When I think: man, I think
sweet potato, popo, ca ca, head, papa,
and the '1' of the little breath exhaling to animate all that.
Sweet potato necessity of the pot of being which *maybe* will have its potful.
And after sweet potato: caca, breath of the double-you see, if you please, of the dungeons of necessity.
The man they can bust and bury when they haven't incinerated him in the baptismal fonts of being.
For to baptize is to cook a being against his will.
Naked by being born and naked by having died, this man whom they've cooked, strangled, hanged, grilled, baptized, shot and incarcerated, slandered and guillotined ' on the SCAFFOLD of existence,
wham! '
this man eats three times a day baby.
When can he eat in peace?
I mean without a larval vampire in the grooves of his teeth,
for who eats without god and all alone
?

181

For a simple plate of lentils is worth much more than the Vedas, the Paranas, the Brahma-Sutras, the Upanishads, the Ramayana, the Kama-Rupas, or the Tarakyan in terms of attaining the basoon sunk back in the shadows of the deepmost chamber where man the actor belches canons chewing the ocular lentil of the eye off the plate of his suffering — or barks curses when his fibers are dislocated under the scalpel.

When I say:

Shit, fart of my prick

(this fart let go in the grand imprecatory style, while belching under the boots of the police),

when I say: the terrors of life, solitude of my whole life,

caca, solitary confinement, poison, *death breed,*

scurvy of thirst,

plague of urgency,

god responds on the Himalaya with:

Dialectic of science,

arithmetic of your usufruct, existence, suffering, grated bone of the skeleton of life turning against ATZILUTH,

to whom,

myself,

I say ZUT.

*Translated by David Rattray*

# ELECTROSHOCK
## [Fragments]

And so, on the surface of daily life, consciousness forms beings and bodies that one can see gathering and colliding in the atmosphere, to distinguish their personalities. And these bodies form hideous cabals where every eventuality comes into the world to argue against what is beyond appeal.

I am not André Breton and I did not go to Baltimore but this is what I saw on the banks of the Hudson.

I died at Rodez under electroshock.

I died. Legally and medically died.

Electroshock-coma lasts fifteen minutes. A half an hour or more and then the patient breathes.

Now one hour after the shock I still had not awakened and had stopped breathing. Surprised at my abnormal rigidity, an attendant had gone to get the physician in charge, who after examining me with a stethoscope found no more signs of life in me.

I have personal memories of my death at that moment, but it is not on these that I base my testimony as to the fact.

I limit myself strictly to the details furnished me by Dr. Jean Dequeker, a young intern at the Rodez asylum, who had them from the lips of Dr. Ferdière himself.

And the latter asserts that he thought me dead that day, and that he had already sent for two asylum attendants to instruct them on the removal of my corpse to the morgue, since an hour and a half after shock I had still not come to myself.

And it seems that just at the moment that these attendants arrived to take my body out, it gave a slight shudder, after which I was suddenly wide awake.

Personally I have a different recollection of the affair.

But I kept this recollection to myself, and secret, until the day when Dr. Jean Dequeker on the outside confirmed it to me.

And this recollection is that everything which Dr. Jean Dequeker told me, I had seen, but not from this side of the world but from the other, and quite simply from the cell where the shock took place and under its ceiling; although for moments there was neither cell nor ceiling for me, but rather a rod above my body, floating in the air like a sort of fluidified balloon suspended between my body and the ceiling.

And I shall indeed never forget in any possible life the horrible passage of this sphincter of *revulsion* and asphyxia, through which the criminal mob of beings forces the patient in extremis before letting go of him. At the bedside of a dying man there are more than 10,000 beings, and I took note of this at that moment.

There is a conscious unanimity among all these beings, who are unwilling to let the dead man come back to life before he has paid them by giving up his corpse totally and absolutely; for existence will not give even his inert body back to him, in fact especially his body.

And what do you expect a dead man to do with his body in the grave?

At such a time, ' I am you and your consciousness is me,' is what all the beings say: salesmen, druggists, grocers, subway conductors, sextons, knifegrinders, railroad gatekeepers, shopkeepers, bankers, priests, factory managers, educators, scientists, doctors,

not one of them missing at the crucial moment.

Pity that no other dead person outside myself should have returned to confirm the matter, for generally speaking the dead do not return.

The electroshock accomplished, this one didn't run its course, as had the first two.

I felt that it wasn't going away.

And my whole inward electric body, the whole lie of this inward electric body which for a certain number of centuries has been the burden of every human being, turned inside out, became in me like an immense turning outward in flames, monads of nothingness bristling to the limits of an existence held prisoner in my lead body, which could neither get out of its lead coating nor stand up like a lead soldier.

I could no longer be my body, I didn't want to be this breath turning to death all around it, until its extreme dissolution.

Thus wrung out and twisted, fiber on fiber, I felt myself to be the hideous corridor of an impossible revulsion. And I know not what suspension of the void invaded me with its groping blind spots,
but I was that void,
and in suspension,
and as for my soul, I was nothing more than a spasm among several chokings.

Where to go and how to get out was the one and only thought leaping in my throat blocked and secured on all sides.
Every wall of charred meat assured me
it would be neither through the soul nor the mind,
all that is of a former world,
this is what each heartbeat told me.

It is the body that will remain


without the mind,


the mind, i.e., the patient.

   N.B. Cool dry pluton in its encounter with hot black pluton: that's
me.

•

He affirms that his sin
was in wishing a place
in the mother of the fathermother
and bullshitting the holy ghost to render it
favorable to his plans.

This sin consisted of a
temptation visited upon me to pass the breath
of my heart through a tube
to both sides of the surface

to consent to the worm
and to leer of my own free will
like a knifeblade
at my own soft flop
at the flop world
at the total exhibition of the body
in front of a
galastralgical
gluttonous curiosity
bloated on the pus of the notorious father,
white pus of blood curdled in laughter;
and to have taken after this child's sweet laughter
who sacrifices himself for life,
his whole rosy body seized by
love in his altarboy's vestments;
and gives the zob or knob of strength
to the thick being
spreads over the rice
baby who

is laughing at
the surprised blood
of his whole life
as an
eggwhite emptied then
volatized in the
gas of the holy ghost

•

The night of the 10 earthquaked cities,
of the Irish who were dismissed and who returned,
of the 300 houses collapsed,
of the 100,000 corpses left unburied,
of the Tibetans of abominations paid by the saw of the virgin
    mother,
of the mouths gagged and charred,
of the grey-suited beards,
of the newsreel images: vessels opened on the high seas,
losing their crews like tons of cargo
flaming out of their jagged portholes,
then of the anti-flesh inventions,
of sexuality observed over the truncated shoulder
of the dolmen which I myself am when I amass my
slaughtered totems,
which I've just resuscitated

•

It is I who committed suicide one day
and tore my body from myself
and battle against what is left of it
and wish forever to come back to myself

who have founded a false world in the mean time:

•

When consciousness overflows a body, there is also a body detaching
itself from consciousness,
no,
there is a body overflowing the body this consciousness came from,
and the whole of this new body is consciousness:
Think hard and long about someone you. . .

1) the vampire with its arms folded in my left ball

2) the woman with the supported nape

3) the grey devil

4) the black father
        a laying-on of black crablice

5) and finally last night
    at the New Athens
    the great revelation concerning the whole system of forming
    god in the slimey eggwhite of my left ball
    after the revelation of the antichrist abyss.

The life we lead is a front for all which the frightful criminal
filthymindedness of some of us has left us.
A grotesque masquerade of acts and sentiments.
Our ideas are only the leftovers of a breath,
        breath of our choked and trussed lungs.
Which is to say for example that if the arterial tension of man is
12,
    it could be 12 times 12 if it were not constrained and squashed down
some place so as not to surpass this sordid level.

And damned if some physician doesn't come telling me that this is called hypertension and it is not good to be in a state of hypertension.

As for me, I answer that we are all in a state of frightful hypertension,

we can't lose an atom without the risk of immediately becoming a skeleton again; while life is an incredible proliferation,

the atom, once hatched, proceeds to lay another, which in fact immediately explodes another.

The human body is a battlefield where we would do well to return.

Now there is nothingness, now death, now putrefaction, now resurrection: to wait for I don't know what apocalypse beyond that, what explosion of what beyond in order to get straightened out
    with things,

is a dirty joke.

Have to grab life by the balls right now.

Who is the man who decided to live with the notion he was not being fitted for the coffin?

Who, on the other hand, is the man who thinks he still may profit by his own death?

Try as they may to make us believe it, we gain no profit from the notion that we will be dead men, going back to the dead, taking our places in the legion of the dead, letting our limbs separate from our selves, and falling down in a heap in the serical charnal houses (liquids).

One doesn't die because one has to die,

one dies because it is a wrinkle forced on the
            consciousness
            one day
            not so long ago.

For one doesn't die in order to come back and remake one's life, but only in order to give up life and get rid of whatever life one had.

And whoever dies, dies because he wanted the coffin.

He accepted one day this spasm of being put through the coffin —
a forced acceptance perhaps, but effective nonetheless,

and no man dies without consenting to it.

Consciousness lives before birth. It lives somewhere, if only for an hour.

All living consciousnesses have existed, I don't know in what sphere or what abyss.

And these abysms consciousness rediscovers here.

What good in fact would the unconscious be if it were not to contain, in the very depths of itself, this pre-world, which is not one anyway, but merely the old burden, rejected (by others than ourselves), of everything which the consciousness could not or would not allow, cannot or will not admit, not under our own control but under the control within us of this other who is not the double or counterpart of the self, who is not the immanent derma of all that the conscious self envelops, and who is not the being that it is not and will become or will not become, but really and palpably an other, a sort of false spy-glove that keeps it under surveillance from morning to night in the hope that consciousness will put it on.

And this other is no more than what all the others are who have always wanted a finger in every person's consciousness.

Psychoanalysis has written a book on the failure of the old Baudelaire, whose life did not precede him by 100 years but rather by this sort of secular infinity, this secular infinity of time which came back to him when he lost his speech and learned and tried to say it, but who believed him, and who believes the affirmations of great poets who have become sick trying to dominate life? For Baudelaire did not die of syphilis, as has been said, he died from the absolute lack of belief attached to the incredible discoveries he had made in his syphilis and repeated in his aphasia.

When he learned it, then, he tried saying it,

that he had lost one of his selves in Thebes, 4,000 years before Jesus Christ.

And that this self was that of an old king.

When he discovered and tried saying that he was not and never had been Mumbledepeg,

but on the contrary that poet in a paradise alley where they were mending poetry, in Brittany, long before the Druids ever settled there.

And the skeleton of the human cock, against all onomatopoeia and reason, in order to rediscover life, found

a sound without echo or cry,

without shadow or double in life,

without the old yoke of the organ that accounts for the five senses,

one day, much later, when the time came for the consciousness of the masses, and the sound of his poetry was the inert weight of planks, the horrible squishing of those six planks they could never fit his corpse into.

For to cure Charles Baudelaire, it would have been necessary to surround him with only a few organisms

enough

never to be afraid of facing a delirium in order to rediscover truth.

Therefore psychoanalysis was unable not to fear reality, however monstrous it might seem, and not to reject — in the dream-symbols representing it — the whole sadistic machinery of crime, the weaver of a vital stuff which Charles Baudelaire wished to mend, and for the sake of which I ask that, for who knows how much time to come, the few men who are its victims continue, as they are condemned prisoners born to be its *fated* scapegoats.

*Translated by David Rattray*

## THE PATIENTS AND THE DOCTORS

Sickness is one state,
health is only another,
but lousier,
I mean meaner and pettier.

There's no patient who hasn't grown,
as there's no one in good health who hasn't lied one day in order not to have the desire to be sick, like some doctors I have gone through.
I have been sick all my life and I ask only that it continue,

191

room motto, i.e.,
for the states of privation in life have always told me a great deal
more about the plethora of my powers than the middleclass drawing-
AS LONG AS YOU'VE GOT YOUR HEALTH.
For my existence is beautiful but hideous. And it isn't beautiful only
because it is hideous.
Hideous, dreadful, constructed of hideousness.
Curing a sickness is a crime.
It's to squash the head of a kid who is much less nasty than life.
Ugliness is con-sonance. Beauty rots.
But, *sick,* one doesn't get high by opium, by cocaine,
or by morphine.
It's the dread of the fevers you got to *love,*
the jaundice and the perfidy,
much more than all euphoria.
Then the fever, the glowing fever in my head,
— for I've been in a state of glowing fever for the
fifty years that I've been alive —
will give me
my opium,
— this existence —
by which
I will be a head aglow,
    opium from head to toe.
For
cocaine is a bone,
and heroin a superman in the bones,

*Ca itra la sara cafena*
*Ca itra la sara cafa*

and opium is this vault
this mummification of blood vault
this scraping of sperm in the vault
this excrementation of an old kid
this disintegration of an old hole

192

this excrementation of a kid
little kid of the buried asshole
whose name is:
shit, pi-pi,
Con-science of sickness.
And, opium of the father and shame,
shame on you for going from father to son —
now you must get dust thrown back at you
and after suffering without a bed for so long.
So it is that I consider
that it's up to the everlastingly sick me
to cure all doctors
— born doctors by lack of sickness —
and not up to doctors ignorant of my dreadful
states of sickness
to impose their insulintherapy on me,
their health for a worn out world.

*Translated by Jack Hirschman*

## BLOOD-WINCHES
### (Reality)

A man I knew pretty well was putting me on about repressed alcohol and drug instincts, in the center of the spiderwork of facts.

And I asked myself what held him back.

It's a Vodka, he answered me in a dream, that has you in its clutches, and holds me back.

For this way I can go to alcohol to beat it instead of creating another alcohol and, without beating it, forgetting.

And I realized that through the Vodka I could see that the alcohol was a sex.

By dint of sawing and grating with all my being at the center of conspicuous sexuality, I understood that this spiderweb was made of ropes and that these ropes, from the very top of an abyss, were holding me back at that moment.

This abyss was an enormous cell with hollow walls and windows, a mountain disclosing some cracks of air, perhaps some chinks of light.

The breathing of freedom was elsewhere.

Where?

In the puddles of unemployed consciousness; and later on, when *I see them more closely,* I'm going to dope them up with a willpower I'll have some day.

My self nailed down by armorplates.

Making an effort to tear myself away from all these nails, I managed finally to get away from the dream and to enter reality; but, awake, in the true light of the three windows of the ward of the Rodez asylum where I found myself, I didn't know at first and immediately where I was, and I continued to feel lost, wrapped up like an enormous foetus of being in the absolute of that pure sensation, in the envelopment of that placenta of my real self, which one calls eternity: conscious of the subconscious and subconscious of the unconscious.

Outside of space, but inside of time.

But if I no longer was conscious of space, of place, of locus, there remained that consciousness of the space of my body, from head to toe, which was nothing else but the pain of being withheld at that very moment and in this grotesque manner.

And by whom?

By myself, because in my lifetime I've lived through worse things than that of being withheld outside of time and space by the ropes of spidersleep.

(And isn't that consciousness what we mythically call the rope of spidersleep.

Like, if you see a spider on the ceiling or a spider in the morning, it will bring shame.)

Anyhow, a voice inside me said, Where am I?, a voice which I renounced; for I understood that I knew where I was and that I was here, at that point in the state of my body, at that height where my alcohol-body arrived at (after I don't know how many struggles with the space of my own time) my self.

And that whoever was saying, 'Where am I?' was in reality an other, truly and corporeally an other who, in time, had always wanted to consider himself opposed to my eternal and not my temporal self, a kind of adulterated imbecile who had always been dedicated to being in disharmony with the facts, but at the same time living as though he were the humdrum Buddha of their syrupy contemplation.

For etcetera etcetera, Nirvana is etcetera etcetera, more facts and not less facts to fight facts etcetera etcetera.

I felt all the ropes on my hands and I felt one at the tip of my spine making music on the earth which was holding it back, the earth which was nothing more than another point on my spine.

This rope came out and sang by itself.

A hollow sound with a sonorous circumstantial coating of a gold and a blue which, in any case, rubbed me the wrong way

because they weren't authentic:

because the noise that a rope can make from one vertebra to another isn't liturgical gold and blue, is neither euphonical nor liturgical, but fecal, bloody, gravelly.

And it was in this way that, all of a sudden, by struggling within the consciousness of my self, there rose from the depths of my gut a blast, and this blast took the form of beings who threw themselves like madmen on my chains.

And cut them.

Then the walls and the room came back to me, and I understood that in spite of all these efforts of criminal tug o' wars beyond the earth, I was purely and simply here, in the psychiatric ward of Rodez.

And the thought came back to me that there was a spot in Tibet where abject monks use gibbets and winches in a certain valley that they've named The Uterus of the Human Form, and where they claim to hold in chains all the consciousnesses of those men who want to escape their individual notions of man, either on the Physical Plane, or on the organic, intellectual, neurotic, sensual Metaphysical Plane.

And after an incalculable labor of years, they have succeeded in establishing a kind of archetypical anatomy before which, under the iron collars of their law, every born man must bend, on pain of being dissected and asphyxiated by them.

I think that Tibet is the only place on earth where this autocracy of the absolute mind has desired to impose itself, and materially succeeded.

There one can see endless iron collars, vises, gibbets, slip-knots, kneeguards, winches, ropes and garrots; and from temple to temple the monks go around making them function according to principals as old as the sempiternal human routine, like the scansion of a somber music where the interstice is like a meat all prepared to be steam-cooked.

And I think that many dreams brutally transformed into nightmares come from the monkeyshines of a humanity which the monks have never been able to enter.

And wasn't it predicted that before 1950 the hand of the monkey would unhook the secret clockface of history and come face to face with the race of men in order to lay claim to the lofty thundering space of the Race of Reality?

P.S. For isn't it true that in the ceremonial millenial pomp of the Dalai-Lama, the ancient sign of a monkey-hand grabbing a man's testicles indicates from what origin the race of the Lamas believes itself to be *Inborn*?

*Translated by Jack Hirschman*

# DEAR DOCTOR AND FRIEND

It is to all the knowledge you have as a veteran doctor that I address myself. Usually, on principle, *I do not believe in science,* learning bores me silly, and I think that the true scholars are those who, all their lives, were ignorant of their discipline and will unfortunately remember it only on the other side of the grave; true knowledge being a nervous muscular affair which doesn't say a word but, at a given point, makes the necessary gesture that saves those things which *never* had been in the hands of the initiated anyway, but rather in the hands of a handful of modest ignoramuses who happened to be men of good will.

Since I know you, it is to a doctor who has seen thousands of sick men and known how to bring into play that element unknown to most doctors and medicine in general, that I direct myself:

What element?

Something in me was about to say pity, but it isn't that; there is in that word a lack of commiseration that doesn't hold true in your case,

pity seeming to come from the rich, from the well provided-for, who don't suffer and who bestow by chance and haphazardly, like Buddha armed with all the spiritual bounties, or like Christ not crowned with thorns (for as a matter of fact he didn't wear that crown of thorns but rather *fled before* it could be imposed upon him),

that blessed one who gives the poor a quivering, a fleeting commotion; whereas he who has suffered something unique, like truly miserable men do, in remembering it, bestows a kind of commiseration taken from his own misery, without ever placing that misery above himself: I think that there is, in that occult part of the self, like the remembrance of a strong bite, one of those attacks of preexistence that opium has cauterized, that only opium can cauterize. And how?

But, in the first place, what is opium?

One looks at this black, noxious juice that has always made *me* at least think of those terrible puddles that can be seen splashing under coffins; — and there are some who maintain that it is life, the very essence of life, that is contained in this black liqueur, this sort of unclassifiable, multiform and, to my way of thinking, *hybrid* ooze that *takes after* evasion, constraint, embrace, effusion, amplification, multiplication, confusion, obtusion, clarity, headiness, heaviness, opacity, thinness, thickness, levitation, stratification, mass and weight — the way a son *takes after* a father — because it didn't come from a pure, disinterested, detached idea; nor from a stirring, heroic idea of the corporeal *self* of man and his becoming; but rather from an interested, greedy, attached, salacious, lewd and erotic idea of life.

I think that the current opium, the familiar black juice of what is known as the poppy, is the overthrow of an ancient, *uprooting* power which man has rejected,

and those who grew weary of seminal liqueur and its erotic returns of the self to the liqueur of the original sin, flung themselves upon opium, but as though with another salaciousness.

That's why, by using keif (another way of profiting from the poisonous baths of the ancient human salaciousness), opium cures sexual greed. And that's what I hate. What I've always looked for in it, what still makes me think of it, is the hope of finding in it the cure for certain subtle pains which physiological medicine cannot isolate;

which pains form the entrance to the black grater, to the friction of black exigencies en route to the loftiest sublimity.

I mean to say that man tends upward, towards a holocaust of grandeur; and it is there, on the road of these elevations, like automatic *interns,*

that the pain, the ache of not-yet being, of not-yet having reached it, hangs on and demands bodily form. And this bodily form, which cures the pre-natal stress and is like the bloody viscera of a grandeur he's already kicked free of, this man, by straining, by trance-like straining, strikes, and collects with a run of luck the drops of the impossible liqueur that cures whatever has not yet risen.

But the current opium is no longer the pure vestige of that black drop. It, too, has been mixed.

You are the only doctor who knows something of all this, because you have felt it all with the remains of a lacerated heart that another doctor wouldn't have stood for.

But how can you expect the legislators of the drug to see this aspect of the problem?

Yours.

Antonin Artaud

P.S.: Nothing can be explained except by the effusions of the trances of the spine that is behind theater and poetry. But who wants to live on such a level? Nobody.

For who wants to conceive of a theater or a poetry in terms of a thing or an object; who wants to admit that there is no state whatsoever in them, and that in order to point out what theater or poetry is, something happens that is like the still uncreated (let's say) but already *willful* body or character, who takes the place and position of a state — psychology being avoided.

And, in its stead, a vivification of unprecedented realities.

Good.

But what is it I mean precisely?

I mean that what theater and poetry are, in my eyes, are the minimals of reality; and that those furnaces that I call the trance-like effusions of the human spine

*behind* theater and poetry

are like energies in a state of waiting, beyond which, in my eyes, is the only screen and the only valid sieve for that which is real, and that is a reality which, before attaining reality,

does not go through the leap

onto the higher stage of theater

and of poetry

and as a result is a reality of defecation made by and for cowards, thought up, since the beginning of time, by the

ineradicable cowards of life,

the crooked atoms of the ineradicable cowards of life.

But what does all this have to do with opium?

Well, it follows, in that opium is the start of the primary chronic force;

opium occurs

when the latent force, knocking over its own body, rises on high, out of an impetus,

or rather,

clashing like cymbals the 2 breasts of its opposite breath,

it smacks upon itself with the full screw of the creaking hinge of the mass of its own weight, which

(but what are the limits of the weight of the latent, chronic force other than those, one might say, of infinity itself?) —

Now then, if the *temporal* infinite is admitted,
the spatial infinite is not conceivable,
and to evoke the infinite of a strain. . .
So it jilts itself, this opium, it makes the gesture that a certain kind of philosophy calls ascending,
like a solemn, retractible pain,
(pinched memory of a state of need when it is no longer necessary).
But all this is quite specious, quite narrow, quite peculiar, quite sophisticated almost, for such a thrilling and formidable question.

I mean that opium is the corporeal residue of an elevated state that had once been reached by man in fear and in blood; and that in order to understand it, it isn't sufficient to call to mind the ordinary kind of psychological and poetical sublimity, but one should rather invoke a state of burial, the sort of essential passageway leading to the genetic cemeteries of a groundwork where matter itself is tirelessly piled up,

a groundwork which is outside existence and never could have borne such an idea.

Now this groundwork, somewhat hairy perhaps, or at any rate heroic, is that of life itself. And man has suffered nothing except from his having neglected its perhaps suffocating but marvelous intensity: perpetual *irascibility*.

The first time with opium, one wants to break everything, to capture whole cities, to go to war against ideas as formidable as they are finished. Such a state remained confused inside me for a long time, and then one day things became clearer:

I noticed that opium lifted me *toward* something, *against* something I wasn't ready to be against:
the idea of stopping up a dreadful void.
In order to stop it up
it would be necessary to *work*,
to work in a certain way.
Now they say opium makes keif,
and pretty quickly human cowardice *returns*, inciting one to do nothing, to not think,
to not think, but to let one's self go to the so-called new truths, to

the so-called jampacked realities that a *well-incubated* opium offers.
Where one does nothing. One just lets one's self go.

In opium, there are scenes that belong to one's great-grandmother;
I mean opium trails off for days, weeks, months at a time; while
other toxics quickly fade.

Seminal liqueur comes from pain, is a clarifying of the pain that
geniuses feel.

*Translated by Odette Myers*

# HERE WHERE I STAND

Here where I *myself* stand / a man
I stand
what I myself do / a man
I do
there is nothing more
there will never be anything more
        than that.
There is no science, no wisdom,
life has been lost from the day one single thing
became known.
I am not of your world,
mine is on the other side of all that is, knows itself, is
conscious, desires and acts.
It's entirely another thing.
There science, knowledge,
envy, desire and its attractions are unknown.
As for ass, I have never been able to understand how it
could cause an erection, suck with the tongue, fill the cheeks,
wet the ganglions.
It's not only its illusory power of attraction that
I deny
it's the *raison d'être* of what is at bottom and which doesn't exist
except as a windbag attraction, so to speak, thick

and poisonous
like that of the Kingdom of Jesus Christ.

●

*Myself* Antonin Artaud
I am a pure spirit
and I make my body
    rise
looking at it as I do
like all the asses of the holy spirit of God
who believe that man is a double
composed of a
    wellrounded spirit
and then of a body,
    an organism
that is
        regulated
        by the spirit
of master eternity on high.
Now *myself* Antonin Artaud
this *self* who has done these impossible labors of Hercules
here where there is no here
where one advances backwards
and where
        the *self*
is really
what has burned
and become very *chic*
and confident
because of the bruises
of general resistance.
I am *precisely* the only one knowing the something that's in
the precessions of bodies.
What is the body?
It's this
    a–um

           this ah-na
           this a ha
           this ha mah
           this ah-mah
which isn't mä
but lä-h-
which isn't ah ou ha
           but SL —
It isn't worthy of God
to be a body
to have a body.
Who is it who is worthy of being
           SLASHED?
The slasher.
For not making any compromise
           any contact
           even smell
           (above all smell)
with said matter,
and for not being afraid of said matter
in directing things to the mass of black fat
in order to re-enter the black fat
with a will absolutely detached and scorning:
this is the black fat rich with life
and not the holy spirit;
it is there that one is a man
truly a man.
           And then?
Then I have to have
           *a whole*
           *body which*
           which isn't
           a spiritual body
           but a man's body
           which moreover

is *not* a being,
which is the true body
of the absolute slash.
How will this *body* be made?
It will be made in such a way
that the problem of the elimination of matter
will be in it *originally*
    *eliminated*,
without nastiness, without bestiality, without spirituality,
    without the needle work of the initiates.
I am stupid the moment I assume an air of discourse
it is with *my breath*
    and *my breath*
and my hand that I've always made
    my body whole
and *suppressed* every thing
    and every being
    and my breath
does what it does
to stop *the life* of beings
who are not me
and will return to me everything they put on themselves
which my breath makes into the real world and things.

    The machinery
    and the style
    of *its* action,
    I know *them*,
    not better than others
    but
    *I am the only one*
    *to know them*
    *that's all*.
Tremor of delirium swelling with life around
my ego, which is only a speck of dust, the distant shadow of
a vapor facing *myself*.

This quivering
        trembling
        loving
        magnetizing
        magnetic
        warmth
of the magic of human shit
is only a fart of false crap
facing the authentic power
        of myself,
which will be definitively re-instated in me
when I recover my absolute virginity.
This isn't true
because it isn't correct
it isn't me who has lost my virginity.
Because what the hell do I
*myself*
        *Antonin Artaud*
have to do with all this assiness of being
and the *logic of the mind*?
I only know one hazy thing
and I know it very hazily
and that's that

        *myself*
        *Antonin Artaud*
I am the master of things
that it's *myself*
who's made them and makes them
and what I know *now*
is that all things have come out by chance
and that they fancy themselves able not to re-enter
but there is another thing I know
not hazily but lucidly
and that's that things
        *and beings*

ineluctably obey the commandment of my breath
and that any opposition, any detour, ends up in a
frightening
> *shock in* return
> *for all I will.*

No matter what kind of ass I am
I'm always less
than any man alive.
The dead put up a bad fight,
you have to be alive to struggle
and now it's Antonin Artaud
who has the umpteen power.
For he is a living mystery
and it's not the crabs of the mind and beings *crawling on*
him that will stop him from plumbing his depths
and *realizing* himself
> just as he is.

Little yes-men who think about life
believe they think about life
fancy they know what life is
> shit.
> Well,

I stuff the devil who fancies he
knows life between my thighs
and encrust a nail in the cunt of the ear
of the left cheek of his asshole
because he's the living-end of asses.
*I don't believe in anything*
I only believe in one thing
that *my* profound power will not restore me
but will *establish me*
> *myself*
> Antonin Artaud

so as to know myself, *feel myself*, desire myself.
The fact is I have a *hunch* about myself and guess

rather than feel myself
because what I feel in me
       *are the others.*
I *saw* that the world was lost
but one must have time to do one thing to escape *above*
*all and especially the devil.*
The power which will come to me and sweep everything will be
                              nothing more
than the sumtotal of all the shots fired by me for
9 years,
in that there must be a mass important enough to
pass beyond the mass of being.
The mass of power important enough to counterbalance the
mass of being having been constituted,
it will constitute a powder *without precedent and without name,*
strong enough to allow me to set up the passage
          from me to myself
          my present ego to my past self,
Hercules having unhooked humanity.
Now the passage is in myself
in the length of *my* own body
which the ganglionic clots block
       by *scientificism*
       functional physiology
and the beings fancying themselves *set up* in the non-nameable of
the potential of the whole capacity
which one designates by *sigmas.*
Imbeciles who still fancy themselves sustained by the influx of
life, *shit,*
         the imperceptible mind,
who rush into pruritus
and withdraw in order not to be infected
and disease comes out of it anyway
because in *withdrawing* they attain what they have never
yet succeeded in seizing,

which would be my self,
          are asses.

*Translated by Jack Hirschman*

# SEVEN POEMS

## [Fragments]

### I

Do evil
   do evil
    and
   commit many sins
   but do no evil to me
   do not touch me
   do not make me do evil
   to myself
   I shall revenge myself cruelly
   you soil and you injure
      God
   there is nothing left for him to do but lose
   he has already committed every filthiness
      no evil to me
      no evil around me
      no evil where I am *myself*
   let me live
      in a world
         pure
   let me have around
       me
          the pure
      the pure heros

## II

it is me
    Man
who will be the judge
at the last accounting
it is to me
that all the elements
of bodies and things
will come to be referred
it is the state of my
body that shall make
the Last Judgment

## III

The place where you suffer
where you know you suffer
where you feel it
and where systematically
and voluntarily
you maintain the things which you do
and which you eat
in the breast of eternal sadness
without letting them go under cover
in an organ forever useless
where a *being* waits for them

## IV

the beings do not come out in the exterior day
they have no other power than to burst forth in the
        subterranean night where they are made
but for eternity

they pass their time
and the time
it takes them to make
one
such step has never been produced
they have to wait for the hand of Man to take and make them
for only
Man
innate and predestined
has
that redoubtable
and
ineffable
capacity

to leave the human body
to the light of nature
to plunge it alive into the gleam of nature
where the sun will wed it at last


V


Thus there is nothing made more ignobly useless and superfluous
than the organ called heart
which is the dirtiest means which the beings have been able
to invent to pump life into me
the movements of the heart are nothing else than a maneuver
by which the being relieves himself on me for me to take
that which I ceaselessly refuse to take from him
that is to say that is how I live

The beings are that virtually parasitic life which is created
on the margin of the true life
and which ends by having the pretention to replace it

210

the actual life taken by itself
constitutes exactly one of the bifurcations of being
beside the real life
and which ends by forgetting it is false
and ends by pretending to see the real life follow
its ignoble movement

### VI

disguised as
a choice of a
body
I say shit
to everything
   and
      I
        go to sleep

### VII

it is very cold
as though
it was
Artaud
dead
who
breathes

*Translated by Kenneth Rexroth*

# WORKMAN'S HAND & MONKEY HAND

working up from the cellar to the roof
cesspool to asthmatic nose

there goes, there he goes, who is
it, that hired hand or the monkey hand?

the working man, you filthy old monkey. . .

who'll wear hipboots to climb clear of this
shit from cesspool anus to the roof
                    who'll sweat then
                        sweat some more, writhing


in all that clay you thought you created him out of
(you did force him, when you thought you'd force him to be born
                                                        [again
to be born again in yr plagiary of innate essence
yr Being innate by presupposition at the bottom of yr
innateness supposedly above all creatures you
get yr creature comforts forked to you with yr
fecal
monkey hand) dirty old punk
monkey that wd lend yrself to anything at all
but never made anything alone
                        ever
& didnt even know how to make yrself be born
with the tonsure of yr hole
                    god
                    you filthy old monkey
where did yr hand plunge into the mildewed
pus of that being who
was fucked by the crime you committed
when he tried to resemble you
                    god?
but WHEN did yr hand ever bleed where the prisoners are being
                                        [flayed alive?
                god?
who was it gnashed his shoulderbones as if

to crawl on all fours
over his own gangrened skeleton

                    god?

you lousy faggot you crotch
full of stars (who
made the lice you're infested with

                    shine?

Yr old man Man or was it you the
Ancient of Days you filthy old cocksucker?)
who ever could earn a human hand
over the shadow of yr innate hand
workman or chimpanzee?
the workman, I'd rather guess

                    god?
                    oh god

who is it knows his own hands
from the bottom of his wellproportioned toes
to the sinus of the fingers of his nose?
you, or he who sweated it out
long before yr eternity

                    god?

and it was hard labor made him human


yes it was almost the perfect crime
you perpetrated against him
who digged in the earth for you & let
you grope all around in his funky sweat
with a withered fecal hand
that monkey hand amputated from the human


who ever shared his hatred
of that cross you've
always wanted to fuck me in the ass with
                    god?

213

& the stale donut of yr ass
you cornhole punk
you old shit ass
you tonsured hole

you tonsured old punkhole
& the stale donut of yr ass
& the circle of yr bungsoul
you corny old bunghole
& the circle of yr grunting
bunghole soul
that soul
you wanted to slip into me
from the bottom of yr bunghole
you tonsured old funkhole
& the stale donut of yr ass

& the circle of yr grunting
                              soul
you wanted to slip into me
from the bottom of yr bunghole
you tonsured old fuckhole
& monkey hand with the hairy wrist

when your
monkey hand w/ the fairy wrist
was gathering all the filth you had
hung in clusters
down your ass
in order to make me
throw it up
              whole

*Translated by David Rattray*

# YOU HAVE TO BEGIN WITH A WILL TO LIVE

You have to begin with a will to live
and not to die
or be dead

seminal life caught in the throat
and conducted between thighs

of a eunuch
for eating
to be man
to be woman

*life is a costume grafted to a dead tree*
that will awaken after death
among the dead

and what was it made of, this
life?

God is what my snotrag's made of

yo  pendor
rara pen nadma
rar pen da panama

teardrop of a larva
larva of teardrop in this
so-called *largo* of
life
in which it's pleased god to see the element of life
he swiped in passing
as he might swipe some flaming clam or oyster
in the fulness of their
ignition

with which they have clothed themselves
and tried *to clothe me*
after having assassinated me.

Being is a lie
man is a lie
a baller of swine
a swine of balls

Beings have invented life
then grafted it
on the dead tree which was all there was

life is a lower form of matter
        *a sub-element*

I was an old carved-up tree
who didn't eat
didn't drink
didn't breathe
but whole snot-feces and jissom-
diarrhea brotherhoods
insinuated themselves in me
enveloping my least filament
and setting up for themselves a sub-elemental
cesspool life
a perjured double of life
which they attempted to animate in lieu of my own
which they were ignorant of
and remain ignorant as ever of its
true movement
pulse and trajectory

the element of true duration

This swarming up of gutter roaches on the death tree I shall never
cease being
shall cease with the *pain* it has brought
enthroned in my whole body
which was no more than the perverse extension
of this pang of orgasm
it had sharpened between my two thighs
in the subsidiary muscle it had *wound up*
to meet the needs of its vile hunger
for hunger, appetite, taste, the need to be nourished
stem solely from this vile orgasm muscle
with which being made love

and was therefore split into man and woman
male and female
whereas there had been no sex in the beginning
while the present body is merely an estrangement
of little breadth
applied to the bark of the terrible tree
that has not ceased growing
and soon will have attained its fatal development

Then there will be the terrible explosion
which will make armies of
lice fart in the distance
for the reason for existence
hasn't yet been pronounced or enunciated
Personally I am terribly bored with being alive
and I shall necessarily quit this life
for not only has the very axletree of life been faked
and displaced
but there can be no axis in this miasma of shit-drizzle
one whiff of which
weighs on a place human beings call
spleen

217

while they pick snot out of their noses
in another little bag they swiped while swarming up
and to which they've given the surname
liver
so as not to forget
the bestial appetites
by which they were born

just a little chance bacteria
which I've passed my time by destroying
since they proliferated on one of my sides
one day when I was asleep
but the sleeper that I am
will not fail to awaken
and I believe this may be very soon

    no ezer
    e nabo
    numiniama
    et niamini
    maniaminia
     uma

*Translated by David Rattray*


## IT HAPPENS THAT ONE DAY

It happens that one day
where I was at
and the way I was

I was no longer virgin
   nor intact
   nor free
   nor alone

nor at the beginning
nor the beginning itself

and while I was still myself
the impurity of beings had covered me
and fastened itself to the beginning;
so I said
that in thought there was no beginning,
and that I myself was the beginning, in my body,
and as for the impurities that cover me, I'll tidy them up
with a whiskbroom.

The thing is, there is no mind to get outside my body to
indicate what it is,
no thought with regard to the acts of my body,

my body actions held within their own limits, alone,
without radiation
or
    substance
or the
       flowering
of thought,

which is the spot where sin fastened on to ruin me
by creating a remorse in me:

to do or not to do
to be or not to be
all manners of posing the problem of life outside the body in a
space that is problematical, illusory, imaginary, etc.

That which is beautiful
will be made beautiful in trees, in flowers, in grass

*but in thought, never;*
and even in trees, in flowers, in grass it is yet to be seen.

All that is of the *space* of imagination and uncreated conception.
And ' uncreated ' means pure nothing.

*Translated by David Rattray*

## THE MISTAKE IS IN THE FACT . . .

The mistake is in the fact that a being is created
*above and beyond the body*

and that it shivers
in a pillar of soot
and scrapings
fashioned of filthy desires entirely,
projections of the lemur mind of the dead,
of the dead one,
of all the dead
mirrored on the esophagal tongue of the living,
that gargoyle gutter of the living
(Oh problem,
it is only at the hour of judgement that the problem
at last will be born,
that the problem suspended for eternities
but never solved
at last will be posed
in its
(pockets)
mere banging shutters,
the TNT
the cheddite
that human beings never have been willing to be,
will come for each one and track him down;

for the senility of the dead has reigned over the living,
has tempted all the living by persistent
tenacious emanations
from the mass of dead minds assembled in a single body
which has been kept where?

Exactly where the priests of Iran, Afghanistan, Lithuania
and China would, could and did keep it;
they, therefore, being the responsibles in this unspeakable delay;
for the bodies of live men do not behave the same
way,
but the fact is, there are no live men,
the whole earth having passed over to the dead

To this foul pillar

Which is why I am a man tyrranized by the lewd priests
of Iran, Afghanistan, Lebanon, Lithuania,
the Caucasus, the Carpathians, who uphold

the meaty skeleton
of abominable man,
a skeleton
with these surloins of meat that are the buttocks

the teats
the calves
the paunch

(the cleavage of the backside
the cheeks
the tongue
the earlobes
the inside flesh of the leg
the vaginal uterine chops of the loins
the auriculation of the tongue and gums

etc. etc.)

All this in an iron cage situated in a cave in the earth
where the so-called initiates will cultivate and cook
the dermal man to
flesh —
fibers of wood.

*Translated by David Rattray*

# I HATE AND RENOUNCE AS A COWARD . . .*

I hate and renounce as a coward every so-called sensate being.

I hate and renounce as a coward every being who is only willing
to be for being's sake and does not want to live to work.

I'd rather work than feel myself alive.

I hate and renounce as a coward every being who consents to having
been created and does not wish to have recreated himself,
    i.e., who agrees with the idea of a god, at the origin of his being
as at the origin of his thought.

I hate and renounce as a coward every being who agrees not to have
been self-created, and who consents to and recognizes the idea of
a matrix nature as the world of his already created body.

I do not consent to not having created my body myself, and I hate
and renounce as a coward every being who consents to live without
first having recreated himself.

I hate and renounce as a coward every being who does not recognize
that life is given him only to recreate and reconstitute his entire
body and organism.

---

*A variant text.

I hate and renounce as a coward every being who does not recognize an authoritarian organism at the origin of his proper personal being, as at that of his entire body.

I hate and renounce as a coward every being who is unwilling to consecrate his whole life to the control as well as to the reorganization of the buried, unfounded and uncreated being of his thought.

I hate and renounce as a coward every being who is quite unwilling to live with sensations, notions, ideas that the body and being imposed upon him in advance, and who is unwilling to consent to live only to recreate himself as much in his whole anatomy as in the reconstitution of his thought.

I hate and renounce as a coward every being who admits to a difference, of notion and being of substance, between the very body of his being and that of his entire mind.

I hate and renounce as a coward every being who agrees to any difference whatsoever in perception between the being of his being and that of his entire mind.

I hate and renounce as a coward every being who separates what he calls his body from what he calls his consciousness or his thought.

I hate and renounce as a coward every being who agrees in advance to merge, a day or an instant beforehand, in the mass-mind.

I hate and renounce as a coward every being who does not agree that life is given him only to separate himself from the masses.

I hate and renounce as a coward every being who will not consent to go through two hundred thousand reincarnations on earth until he finally becomes conscious of having been born.

I hate and renounce as a coward every being who does not agree that the consciousness of having been born is a search and a study superior to that of living in society.

I hate and renounce as a coward every being who is unwilling to pass his life in order to create it two hundred thousand times over, and to recreate the control of his life in the body of society.

I hate and renounce as a coward every being who allows he can live without having first been invited to.

I hate and renounce as a coward every being who consents to give himself over to the sensations of being, without first having controlled and verified them.

I hate and renounce as a coward every being who does not agree that being is granted him in order to verify for himself the validity of life in a created being.

I hate and renounce as a coward every being who consents to live without giving himself over to the control and the exclusive search for the validity of the created breath.

I hate and renounce as a coward every being who can believe himself anything but a body created to separate its validity from the life of any other created body.

I hate and renounce as a coward every being who can endure to live without first having separated himself in truth and essence from an already created organism, whether individual, unitary or totalitarian.

I hate and renounce as a coward every being who cannot think that the search for his life as a being is a study superior to that of giving himself over to sensations, to principals, or to notions uncontrollably lent by other personalities.

I hate and renounce as a coward every being who is quite willing to live without first having verified the validity, the truth, the personal application and the character of the sensation thus lent.

I hate, furthermore, and renounce any being who is willing to put up with lending himself to these totalitarian applications of crablice.

Finally, I hate and renounce as a coward every being who can think that the application to these totalitarian scratching sensations is superior to the verification and control of his own search for life in defiance of these unleashed tornadoes of crablice.

To conclude, I hate and renounce myself as a coward if I think that the joy of these totalitarian kicks is superior for me to the act of tearing myself loose from their uncontrollable rotations.

I shall be chaste and pure,
virgin, intact, untouchable

I shall touch no being

I, Artaud

I hate and renounce all mind and god.

I shall be chaste for eternity.

I shall be a virgin for eternity.

I hate and renounce all mind and god.

I have strength because I have strength,
but I hate and renounce as a coward any being who doesn't want to earn it.

I hate and renounce as a coward every sensation and every being.

I hate and renounce the so-called sensations of being.

I am by essence clean and pure.
I am pure because I am clean.
I am clean because I am pure.

I hate and renounce as a coward every sensation one might wish to substitute for an act.

                  a Erto shaba shaliera
                  Ba shaliera renvoo
                  o o erto
He who invented this language isn't even ' me.'

We are not yet born,

we are not yet of this world,

there is no world yet,

things have not been created,

the *raison d'être* not yet found,

the only question is that of having a body,
of having with oneself enough body to tear one's strength loose from other beings who have stolen it.

I speak for myself.
I am answerable to no one in the organization.

Get back down in your grave god you lowdown corpse.

There remains to be solved the question of the composition of the human body, of the localization of its organs
and of its elements.

Men will tear from themselves the liquid, the viscous, the slack, the cowardly.

*Translated by David Rattray*

## THERE'S AN OLD STORY

There's an old story about charred monkeys keeps coming
    back
to me when I think about the stories of this collapsing world
    I am
still a tenant of, though not for
long I hope
where the few real friends I have, friends not so much of
my work as of my life, give the effect of a last small
island of consciousness
aboard the ark, even if we suppose that this means nowadays
some mere raft of flesh & bones,
so:
aboard the ark on the eve of the big splash, on the verge of
strangulation,
asphyxia of putrid meat rushing up over the
brain mind
& smothering it.
A frightful wrath leaps up on every side, where,
I do believe, the big social problems are nothing much
next to a certain physiological irritation in the epidermis
skin & bones, something very few have seen
that will drown out all else soon,
for this is no mere rage of the mind,
not even a rage of the heart, no,

this time we have a body rage
the rage of this great stepchild of the history of
man as well as beast:
the  b o d y .
Many big splashes went down the drain of history,
many inexpiable disasters that stopped short and
however inexpiable they may have felt
agreed to throw in the sponge
because the body was always
being kept out of the rumble
& it was mind, not body, that ran those revolutions
AS IF revolution were a thing that got
underway then stuck to the rules
like a ballet or the pawns on a
checkerboard
& you finally tucked it away in your coat pocket
like the pawns on a
checkerboard.
So, as long as history has been history, mind not body has
led the ballet — no corps even in the corps du ballet.
The mind with its monopoly on values & things
which upsets all value of things
AS IF there were ideas & things, with even
the body being submitted to a ploughshare, plus
ideas & principles — and
a body that is supposed to be Idea.
So that I Artaud suspect I am a horse & not a man
I am not that suspect on all fours being kicked in irons
now & then, but I am a certain being so iron in force
no horse could suspect I was a man
nor any man force me up, once on all fours.
So certain I was I was a horse
I made & nailed on
4 iron shoes
being no man but a certain horse kicked

by all who suspect I am a man & so force me
not to be a horse that I am forced
up in the air with all 4 edges flying & I can
kick like hell
& snort out both nostrils
& they can't trip me up on words because I
won't be saying anything.
And what am I trying to say now:
WHAT THE FUCK AM I HERE FOR?

*Translated by David Rattray*

## THE HUMAN FACE

The human face
is an empty power, a
field of death.
The old revolutionary
claim to a form
that's never corres-
ponded with its body, goes off
to be something other
than the body.
So it's absurd
to reproach a painter
for academically
insisting in his time upon
still reproducing
the features of the human face
such as they are; for such
as they are, they haven't
yet found the form they
point to and specify
to make more than a sketch;
but from morning to evening

and in the midst of ten thousand dreams
they churn as if in the
crucible of a never-
wearying passional throb.
Which means
that the human face
hasn't yet found *the* face
and that it's up to the painter
to give it it.
But that means
the human face,
such as it is, is still in quest of it-
self with two eyes a
nose a mouth
and the two auricular
cavities
which correspond to the holes
of the sockets like
the four openings
to the sepulcre of
approaching death.
The human face
in effect carries a kind
of perpetual death
with it
from which it's really up to the painter
to save it
by giving it back
his own peculiar features.
In effect after countless thousands of years
that the human face has spoken
and breathed
one still has the impression
that it hasn't even begun to
say what it is and what it knows,

and I don't know a painter in
the history of art, from Holbein
to Ingres, who has succeeded
in making that face of
man speak. The portraits
of Holbein or of Ingres are
thick walls revealing
nothing of the ancient mortal architecture
supporting itself under the
arcs of the arches of the eyelids
or molding itself
in the cylindrical tunnel
of the two mural
cavities of the ears.
Only Van Gogh
has extracted from a human
head a portrait
that is the
rocket explosive of
the beating of a burst
heart.
His own.
The head of Van Gogh in
a soft hat renders nul
and void
all the attempts of abstract
painters that could be
made, from his time to the
end of eternity.
Because that avid butcher
face, thrown out like
a cannonshot on the most
extreme surface of the canvas
and which all at once
finds itself stopped short

by a void eye,
and returned to the inner world,
thoroughly drains all
of the most specious
secrets of the abstract world
where the non-figurative painter
can delight, —
in the portraits
I have drawn
I have above all avoided
forgetting the nose the mouth
the eyes the ears or
the hair, but I've sought
to force the face that was
talking to me to reveal
the secret
of an old human story
which was
taken for dead in
the heads
of Ingres or Holbein.
Occasionally I've summoned
objects trees
or animals to come near
the human heads because
I'm still not sure
of the limits by which the
body of my human
Self may be stopped.
Moreover I've definitely
broken with the art
style or skill in
all the drawings that one
will see here. I mean
there'll be trouble for those who

consider them
works of art,
works of aesthetic
simulation of reality.
Not one
properly speaking is a
work
All are sketches,
I mean
soundings or
gropes
in all the directions
of accident, of possibi-
lity, of chance or of
destiny.
I haven't sought
to take great pains with my lines
or their effects
but rather to inventory the
kinds of patent
linear truths which
are as valid
through words,
through written phrases,
as through the graphism
and perspective of lines.
It is in this way that several drawings
are a mixture of poems and
portraits
of written interjections
and plastic evo-
cations of fundamental
materials of human
beings or animals.
And in this way you have to accept

these drawings in the
barbarism and disorder
of their
graphic manner ' which is
never preoccupied with
art ' but with the sincerity
and the spontaneity
of the stroke.

(written for a presentation of his
*Portraits and Drawings* at the
Galerie Pierre, July 4-20, 1947)
*Translated by Jack Hirschman*

## THE INDIAN CULTURE

I came to Mexico to make contact with
    Red Earth
and she stinks as she smells sweet
and she smells good when she is stinking.

    Aboriginal urine down the slope of a
                tight vagina
    that objects when you grab it.
    Urinary camphor from the eminence of a
                dead vagina
    boxing your ears when you spread it,

when you gaze from the height of Mirador
                              of Pitre,
the studded tomb of the terrible father,
the hole hollowed out, the tart sunken
      hole where the cycle of red lice boils,
that cycle of solar red lice
all white in the network of veins
      of one of the two of them.


But which two, and which one of them?
What two
      at the time
      slandered seventy times over
      when man
                        crossbred with himself
      giving birth to a son
      by the sodomy
      of his own
      hardened ass.
So, why two of them
and why, in the first place, TWO?


      Pitiful clown of a papa's mimicry,
            filthy parasite mountebank in the hollow
      mamaloaf pulled from the fire!


For all the round suns spending around you
are nothing next to the clubfoot
with its immense articulation of the old
gangrenous shank, old
ossuary gangrenous shank where
a buckler of bone ripens,
a war-like underground rising up of
the buclers of all the bones.

What does that mean?
It means that papamummy stop buggering
the innate pederast,
the filthy bucker of christian orgies,
the interloper between ji & cry
who was contracted in jiji-crycry;

and that means war
will replace the fathermother
here where the ass built its barrier
against the nourishing plague
of the Red Earth buried
under the corpse of the dead
warrior
who was afraid of going through
the periplum of the serpent
that bites its tail from up front
while papamummy make
little fanny bloody.

And looking at it from up close,
within the cankered shank of a slice of
the old blotchy femur,
they're falling this way and that way, stinking;
and the old warrior rises up
with his insurgent cruelty,
with that unspeakable cruelty
for life without there being
existence to justify you;

and into the fixed hole of earth
seen from above and within,
all the enlightened tips of tongues are falling
which thought themselves souls one day
without even being volitions;

and they are raising all the whipcracks of
                    my dead hand
         against the uplifted tongue
         and the sexes of desire,
         who are only verbal dice
         powerless to seize existence;

    yet they're falling brighter than the suns
         beamed into the cave where
         papamummy and fairy son
         have been killing each other since
         before it all started stinking.

When the solar jackass thought himself

                              well and good.

         And when is it
                  the heavens are in
                              their circle?
When one is
         outside it,
    supremely dumb
                  to smell it
                        in his cunt,

with nothing to stand as a barrier against
                  the void,
where there is neither horizon nor upright,
nor surface
nor height,
and everything puts you back in touch with the depths,
    when one is straight all the length of him long.

                    *Translated by Jack Hirschman*

237

# HERE LIES

I, Antonin Artaud, am my son,
    my father, my mother,
    my self;
    leveller of the imbecile periplum rooted
    to the family tree:
    the periplum papamummy
    and infant wee,
              crud from the ass of
                     granmummy
      much more than pa and ma.

      Meaning:
before mummy and papa,
who didn't have a pa and ma,
          as said,
(and where would they have gotten
        them
when they became that unmatched
        pair
neither husband nor wife
has been able to see, sitting or standing)
before this improbable hole
that the mind plumbs to find for us,
           to disgust

us a little more with ourselves
for being this useless body
made of meat and wild sperm,
hanging, since before even the lice,
sweating on the impossible table
of the sky
      its horny stink of atoms,
      its randy stink of abject
*detritus*
expelled from the sleep of the Inca

238

with mutilated fingers

    who for an idea had an arm
    but only a dead palm for a
    hand, having lost his fingers
    killing kings.

       ●

Driving the iron cymbals now
I take the low road, gouging
into the gullet of the right eye

under the grave of the taut plexus
that makes an elbow in the road
to let the lawful child go free

      NUYON KIDI
      NUYON KADAN
      NUYON KADA
      TARA DADA II
      OTA PAPA
      OTA STRAKMAN
      TARMA STRAPIDO
      OTA RAPIDO
      OTA BRUTAN
      OTARGUGIDO
      OTE KRUTAN
   for I was Inca but no king
      KILZI TRAKILZI
      FAILDOR
      BARA BAMA
      BARABA
      MINCE
   etretili
      T I L I
  getting goosed in the golden
       pantaloons

> through the rout and ruins,
>> to the very core.

And there was no sun and no person,
no one ahead of me no one before me
no one no one no one to thou me.
I had a few faithful who never stopped
> dying for me.
When they were too dead to go on living
they left only the despicable ones,
the same who coveted their ranks
while fighting alongside them,
too cowardly to fight against them.
But who else saw them?
> no one.

Myrmidons of Infernal Persephone,
microbes of every hollow gesture,
spittle buffoons of a dead law,
cysts ravishing among themselves,
tongues of the avaricious
forceps
scratched through their own
>> urine,
latrines of the bony dead
always sapping the same
bleak
> vigor
from the same fire,
>> from whose cave
the contriver of a terrible
> knot,
holed-up with
motherlife is
the viper eating
my eggs.

●

For it's the end which is the beginning
and this end
is the end
that wipes away
every means

●

And Now,
let me tell you,
all of you, you've always
made me shit.
Why don't you go
fuck
a prickly
pussy
crablice
of eternity.

Never again will I have anything to do
with the ones who swallowed
the iron stud of life.

One day soon after I lost my mamatit
I met up with the ones who swallowed
the iron stud of life,
and one of them wrestled me under him
and god poured me back to it
(THE BASTARD)

So that's how they
yanked papamummy
and the fryingfat of ji in
Cry
out of me,

out of the sex (the center)
of the great strangulation,
from which was yanked this cross

                                    -ing of the bier

(dead)
and of the substance
that brought life
to Jizo-cry
when the blood

                                    was sucked from
                                            the droppings

of my dead *self*

                       and all fake life
                       browned itself on the outside,


and that's how:
The grand mystery of the Indian culture
is to bring the world back to zero
ALWAYS


but I'd just as soon say
        1) better too late than too soon
        2) meaning
           sooner
           than too soon
        3) meaning
           the latest
           can come back only if
           sooner ate too soon
        4) meaning
           at the same time the latest
           precedes
           too soon
           and the soonest
        5) and no matter how fast

soonest is,
too late,
who doesn't say a word,
is always there
dissonanting, point by point,
all the soonests.

*Commentary*:
They came, all the bastards,
after the great dissonance
sounded from top to bottom
    1) eggface

              (shh, whisper this)
    didn't you know
    that the state of
        EGG
            was the antiartaud

    state
    par excellence,
    and for poisoning artaud
    there's nothing
    like whipping up
    a good omelette
    in the spaces
    targeting in on the
    jelly bullseye point
    that artaud,
    seeking to make Man,
            has fled
    like a horrible plague,
    and it's this point
    they put back in him
    — nothing, I say, like a good stuffed **omelette**
    poison cyanide and capers
    hurled through the air to his zone

to discombobulate artaud
in the anathema of his bones

## HANGING FROM THE
## INNER CADAVER

and 2) *palelark puuuling*
*larglark cawwling*

3) *tuban tit tarting*
with the head of
the head ogling you

4) *homonculus frontal*
*punch*
*from the pinch whoring you*
rocking to the stinking boss
this arrogant capitalist
from limbo
swimming toward the stickisome trinity
of fathermother with kiddy sex
to empty the body whole,

wholly of its vitality
and put in its place . . . who?
he who was made by Being and Nothing-
ness,
the way one puts a baby to make peepee.

## AND THEN THEY ALL GOT
## THE FUCK OUT OF THERE

No. What's left is this awful gimlet,
this gimlet crime,
this awful

244

old stud of a screwed-up
deviation to the profit of the son-in-law
[but don't they see that the fake son-in-law
is Jizi-cry,
already known in Mexico
long before his flight to Jerusalem on a
jackass,
and the crucifixion of Artaud at Golgotha.
Artaud
who knew that there was no mind
but only body
which is remade like the broken dentures of
the gears of a corpse
in the gangrene
of the femur
*within.*

All true language
is incomprehensible
like the click
of clack teeth
or the clap (whorehouse)
of the femur grinding (bloody)]
fake, as the son-in-law is,
from the pain sawed from the bone

DAKANTALA
DAKIS KETEL
TA REDABA
TA REDABEL
DE STRA MUNTILS
O EPT ENIS
O EPT ATRA

from the pain
sweating
*inside*

THE BONE.

From the pain mined from the bone
something was born
and became that mind
so as to scrape around in the sorrow driven
by pain,
       this womb
a concrete womb
             and the bone
             from the depths of stone
             become bone.

*Moral*:
    Don't ever push yourself more than you need
    to build a culture on the weariness
    of your bones.

*Moral*:
    When the stone was eaten by the bone
    that the mind nibbled from behind,
    the mind opened its trap too wide
    and received in the behind
                   of its mind
    a kick that withered its bones.

          Then

          *then*
          then
          bone by bone
        the everlasting levelling returned

AND TURNED THE ELECTRIC ATOM
TO DISSOLUTION POINT BY POINT.

*Conclusion*:

As for me, uncomplicated
Antonin Artaud,
no one can touch me
when one is only a man
　　or

　　　　　　　god.
I don't believe in father
　　　　　　in mother,
got no
papamummy

nature
mind
or god
devil
body
or being
life
or nothingness,
nothing inside or out
and above all no mouth to mouthe Being,
that sewer drilled with teeth
where man, who sucked his substance
from me, looks at me all the time
waiting to get hold of a papamummy
and remake an existence
free of me
over and above my corpse
taken
　　from the void
　　　　　　itself,
and sniffed at
　　　　from time
　　　　　　　to time.

247

         I speak
                  from above
                           time

as if time
were not fried,
were not this dry fry
of all the crumbles
at the beginning
setting out once more in their coffins.

                *Translated by F. Teri Wehn & Jack Hirschman*

# Artaud Bibliography

*Compiled by Daniele Robert*

## 1921

' L'atelier de Charles Dullin ' (Chroniques); ' La Bouteille et le Verre,' ' Verlaine boit,' ' Mystagogie,' ' Madrigaux,' (poèmes), in *Action*, No. 6.

' L'Antarctique ' (poème), in *Action*, No. 10.

## 1922

' Bar Marin,' ' Aquarium,' (poèmes), in *Action*, mars-avril.

## 1923

*Douze Chansons* (Maurice Maeterlinck: prologue d'Artaud), Collection Les Contemporains, Stock, Paris.

*Tric-trac du ciel* (poèmes), Galerie Simon.

## 1924

' Boutique de l'Ame ' (poème) in *CAP*, No. 1.

## 1925

' Sur le Suicide,' in *Le Disque Vert*, No. 1.

' Le Mauvais Rêveur,' in *Le Disque Vert*, No. 2.

' Avec moi dieu-le-chien, et sa langue,' ' Poète Noir,' ' L'arbre,' ' La Rue,' ' La nuit opère,' ' Vitres de son,' (poèmes) in *Le Disque Vert*, No. 3.

' Texts surréalistes,' ' Réponse à l'enquête sur le Suicide,' ' Rêves,' in *La Révolution Surréaliste*, No. 2.

' L'activité du Bureau de recherches surréalistes,' ' Lettre aux Recteurs des Universités Européennes,' ' Adresse au Pape,' ' Adresse au Dalai-Lama,' ' Lettre aux Ecoles du Bouddha,' ' Lettre aux Médecins-Chefs des asiles de fous,' in *La Révolution Surréaliste*, No. 3.

*Le Pèse-Nerfs*, suivi de Lettres de ménage (couverture d'André Masson), impr. de Leibovitz, Paris.

*L'Ombilic des Limbes*, NRF Gallimard, Paris.

*L'Ombilic des Limbes*, suivi des fragments d'un Journal d'Enfer, éditions des *Cahiers du Sud*, Marseille.

'Nouvelle lettre sur moi-mème,' in *La Révolution Surréaliste*, No. 5.

'La vitre d'amour,' in *La Revue Européenne* [N.D.]

### 1926

'L'Enclume des forces,' 'Invocation à la Momie,' (poème), in *La Révolution Surréaliste*, No. 7.

'Lettre à la voyante,' 'Uccello le poil,' in *La Révolution Surréaliste*, No. 8.

### 1927

*A la grande nuit, ou le Bluff surréaliste*, Paris (l'auteur).

*Correspondance avec Jacques Rivière*, NRF, Gallimard, Paris.

*Point final*, Paris (l'auteur).

### 1928

'Le clair Abélard,' in *Les Feuilles Libres*, dec. 1927-janv. 1928.

'L'Osselet Toxique,' in *La Révolution Surréaliste*, No. 7.

### 1929

*L'Art et la Mort*, Denoël, Paris.

### 1930

*Le Théatre Alfred Jarry et l'Hostilité Publique* (en collaboration avec Roger Vitrac), Paris.

### 1933

'Le théatre de la cruauté,' in *14 Rue du Dragon*, No. 2.

'Le temple d'Astarté,' in *14 Rue du Dragon*, No. 4.

'Le vieillesse précoce du cinéma,' in *Les Cahiers Jaunes*, No. 4.

### 1934

*Heliogabale ou l'Anarchiste Couronné*, Denoël et Steele, Paris.

### 1937

*Les Nouvelles Révélations de l'Etre*, Denoël, Paris.

**1938**

*Le Théatre et son Double,* Gallimard (collection ' Métamorphoses '), Paris.

**1944**

*Révolte contre la Poésie* (amis de l'auteur), Paris.

**1945**

*D'un Voyage au Pays des Tarahumaras,* éditions de la Revue ' Fontaine,' Paris.

**1946**

*Lettres de Rodez,* impr. G. L. Mano, Paris.

*Xylophonic contre la Grande Presse et son Petit Public* (' Histoire entre le Groume et Dieu ' par A. Artaud; ' Apoème ' par Henri Pichette) impr. Davy, Paris.

' Le Théatre et l'Anatomie,' in *La Rue,* (Juillet).

' Les Mères à l'Etable,' in *L'Heure Nouvelle.*

' Centre-Noeuds,' in *Juin No. 18* (Juin 18).

' Lettre sur Lautréamont,' in *Cahiers du Sud,* No. 275.

**1947**

*Portraits et Dessins* (poème de l'artiste), Galerie Pierre, Paris.

*Artaud le Momo* (illustré de 8 dessins de l'auteur), Bordas, Paris.

*Ci-git, précédé de la Culture Indienne,* impr. D. Viglino, Paris.

*Van Gogh, le suicidé de la société,* K éditeur, Paris.

' Les Malades et les Médecins,' in *Les Quatre Vents,* No. 8.

' L'aveu d'Arthur Adamov,' in *Cahiers de la Pléiade,* avril.

' Main d'Ouvrier,' ' Coleridge le Traitre ' et ' Il Faut Avoir L'Envie de Vivre,' in *Revue K,* No. 1.

**1948**

*Pour en Finir avec le Jugement de Dieu,* K éditeur, Paris.

*Ci-Git, précéde de la Culture Indienne,* K editeur, Paris.

*Le Théatre de Séraphin,* collection ' l'air du temps,' Paris.

' Aliéner l'Acteur ' et ' Le Théatre et la Science,' in *L'Arbalète,* No. 13.

'Introduction à la lecture de son oeuvre,' in *Critique*, (octobre).

'Lettre à Peter Watson,' in *Critique*, (octobre).

'Paris-Varsovie,' in *84*, Nos. 3-4.

'Douze textes inédits,' in *84*, Nos. 5-6.


### 1949

*Supplement aux Lettres de Rodez*, suivi de 'Coleridge le traitre,' G. L. Mano, Paris.

*Lettre contre la Cabbale*, Jacques Haumont, Paris.

'Les dix-huit secondes,' 'La pierre philosophale,' 'Le Théâtre de Séraphin,' 'La où j'en suis,' in *Cahiers de la Pléiade*, (printemps).

'Suppôts et supplications,' (extraits) in *Les Temps Modernes* (février).

'Il y a une vielle histoire de singes carbonisés,' in *84*, No. 7.

'Inédits,' in *84*, Nos. 8-9 et 10-11.


### 1950

*Le Théatre de Séraphin*, Bettencourt, Paris.

(Prével, J. *De Colère et de haine*) Avec un poème par Antonin Artaud, éditions du Lion, Paris.

'La Mort et l'Homme,' in *84*, No. 13.

'Lettre à l'administrateur de la Comédie Française,' in *84*, No. 13.

'Je n'ai jamais rien étudié . . .' in *84*, No. 16.


### 1951

'Suppôts et supplications,' (extraits) in *La Nef* (décembre-janvier).


### 1952

*Lettres* d'Antonin Artaud à J. L. Barrault, Bordas (documents de la revue théatrale), Paris.

(*La Bouche ouverte*, conte de Marcel Béalu) Commenté par A. Artaud, Paris.

'Trois lettres adressées à des médecins,' 'Lettre à la voyante,' 'L'Eperon malicieux,' 'Le Double Cheval,' in *Botteghe Oscure*, No. 8.

### 1953

*Vie et Mort de Satan-le-Feu,* suivi de 'Textes mexicains pour un nouveau mythe,' éditions Arcanes, Paris.

'Trois textes,' *Le Disque Vert,* No. 4.

### 1954

'Le Théatre et la Science,' in *Théatre Populaire* [N.D.]

### 1956

Début de la publication des oeuvres complètes d'Antonin Artaud, Gallimard, NRF (à 1965: Tomes I-V).

### 1957

*Autre chose que l'enfant beau* (pointe-sèche originale de Pablo Picasso), L. Broder, Paris.

### 1959

'Lettre à Pierre Loeb,' in *Antonin Artaud,* par Georges Charbonnier (Poètes d'Aujourd'hui: Seghers, Paris).

### 1960

'Chiote à l'esprit,' in *Tel Quel* (printemps).

*Translations by Artaud:*

1. *LE MOINE* de Monk Lewis (Denoël & Steele, 1931).
2. *CRIME PASSIONNEL* de Ludwig Lewisohn (Denoël & Steele, 1932).
3. 'Le Chevalier Mate — Tapis' d'après Lewis Carroll, *Cahier du Sud,* 1948.